1978:
Rugby league's greatest finals series

Glen Humphries

Last Day of School

ISBN: 978-0-6489911-7-5
1978: Rugby League's Greatest Finals Series is copyright Glen Humphries 2025

For more information email dragstermag@hotmail.com. If you loved this book so much that you want to buy some more copies then head over to my micropublishing site Last Day of School (find it at www.lastdayofschool.net). And maybe buy some copies of my other books. They're good, I promise you. And all so reasonably priced.

This book is copyright. All rights reserved. Except for private study, research, criticism or reviews, as permitted under the Copyright Act, no part of this book may be reproduced, stored in a retrieval system, or transmitted in any form or by any means without prior written permission. That's not too much to ask, is it? Though I guess you don't need to be told that. If you're so interested in this book that you've gone to the trouble of reading the fine print on the copyright page, I'm sure you'll do the right thing.

About the author

Glen Humphries has been a journalist with the Illawarra Mercury for three decades, which he knows makes him seem really old. He is also the author of 17 books – you're holding his 18th. And he shocked himself when he counted them all for this biography. Because, really, he has no idea how he has managed to write so many. Partially because he is a lazy guy who likes nothing more than stretching out on the lounge and doing nothing. He thinks the 1978 finals series is the greatest ever, even if his beloved Dragons played no part in it. He thought about counting the tackles in all the matches in the finals but, frankly, felt it would be too much work. He liked that researching this book gave him an excuse to watch a bunch of old footy matches. For several years in primary school he played rugby league. In his first season, the coach put him on the wing; not because he was fast but because the coach - who was also a teacher at school - didn't know if he was any good. To this day he figures that coach was phoning it in and hated being footy coach on sports days. When he changed school the following year, that coach put him in at lock and made him captain. Obviously, that guy could recognise talent when he saw it. He still regrets never playing in a grand final during his school years. In his 20s he thought about playing league again but realised he had no appetite for getting smashed by people much bigger than him. Glen regrets the cultural shift away from players growing moustaches and believes the NRL should step in and do something.

Published by Gelding Street Press
Aussie Rock Anthems: The Stories Behind Our Biggest Hit Songs
Sticky Wickets: Australian Cricket's Controversies and Curiosities
Jack Gibson's Fur Coat: Rugby League Oddities and Artefacts
Biff: Rugby League's Infamous Fights

Published by Last Day of School and available at www.lastdayofschool.net
Friday Night at the Oxford
Healer: The Rise, Fall and Return of Tumbleweed
Lull City: The Wollongong Music Scene 1955-2020
Alive in the Five: The Steelers' 1992 Premiership Charge
Keira Street: Tales of gunfire, flames, drama, development, dining, music, mayhem, a trouser burglar and a kebab van
The Slab: 24 Stories of Beer in Australia
James Squire: The Biography
Sounds Like an Ending: Midnight Oil, 10-1 and Red Sails in the Sunset
Alright!: Queen at Live Aid
Little Darling: Daryl Braithwaite and The Horses
The Six-Pack: Stories from the World of Beer
Beer is Fun
Night Terrors: The True Story of the Kingsgrove Slasher

To Kim and Josie

1978

Introduction

Labelling anything as 'the greatest of all time" is a dicey exercise. No sooner do you make the pronouncement than people flood in with the what-abouts, insistent that you've got the whole thing wrong. Which will probably happen as a result of the next sentence, but here goes. The 1978 rugby league finals series is the greatest of all time. And my team didn't make the top five that year, so there's no personal bias here.

Sure, there are plenty of great finals memories. There's 1967, when Canterbury ended the Dragons' run of grand final appearances. 1982's Manly-Newtown biff fest. The 1998 comeback by the Dogs against the Eels, where Paul Carige etched his name in footy folklore for all the wrong reasons. Nathan Cleary single-handedly destroying the Broncos in the 2023 GF. You could even throw in 2002, when the Dogs were banned from the finals altogether after rorting the salary cap.

But they're all individual moments from a series. In terms of sheer drama, the 1978 series had it all – from the last round of the regular season all the way through to the big one. There were seven-tackle sets. A team pushing to have a match annulled. Not one but two matches ending in draws and having to be replayed. Greg Hartley. A grand final being played on a Tuesday afternoon. A team hamstrung by having not one, but two star players suspended. The potential for a newly established and already violent rivalry to kick off again. The premiers having to play and win six matches in 23 days while nursing all the bruises so as to keep their best side on the field.

It was a finals series that featured two teams – Parramatta and Canterbury – on the cusp of dominating in the coming decade. There was Manly, looking to solidify their ranking as the team of the 1970s with a fourth title. The men in black and white – Western Suburbs – had shocked everyone by claiming the minor premiership after only a solitary finals appearance in a decade.

Rounding out the top five were the Sharks, the youngest team at just 11 years old and about to make their second grand final appearance; a successful future

1978

seemed on the horizon. Their fans would never have expected they'd wait almost 20 years before they'd be there again (in the Super League decider) and four decades before they'd finally win one.

The 1978 season was the start of a new era of rugby league, and saw the sun setting on another. The sport had just begun to be televised, though in a manner unrecognisable to modern eyes used to seeing every match live every weekend. The ABC screened a Saturday match live while Channel 7 had the exclusive rights to screen a match on Sunday, but forget about seeing it live – you'd have to wait until 6.30pm for an hour of highlights. And pray that the sports reporter on the 6pm news doesn't ruin it by saying who won.

That growth in TV coverage began the slow decline of the era of the biff. Once upon a time the powers that be deemed it quite alright for players to punch each other in the head. That started to change following the televised Wests-Manly clash in Round 7 in 1978. Plenty of punches were thrown and it was all delivered into people's lounge rooms in full colour. The league didn't think that was a good look and so took its first baby steps towards banning the biff; it would take the body until

2019 to finally get there.

The game was still played under the five-metre rule, which allowed the defending team to get into the opponents' backline almost before the dummy half had passed. Looking at it with modern eyes, it's hard to understand how anyone managed to score at all. Scrums were still a contest and likely to result in half of the forwards ending up on the ground while play continued around them. If you wanted to clip someone around the ears with a swinging arm at any stage in the game, there was a good chance you'd get away with it.

The corners of the field were marked with black and white striped cardboard tubes that were sought after by the kids running onto the field after full-time (yes, spectators could actually run onto the field). The goalpost padding looked useless; like someone had wrapped a towel around the base. Injured players were treated by squeezing a wet sponge over the back of their neck. Some would even drink the water from it, leading to illness from the contaminated liquid.

Night football was still a relatively new thing, and players swore by a smear of black goo under each eye. What it actually did was unclear, but every player on the field under floodlights wore the stuff. That we play heaps of night footy these days but you never see that black

1978

goo any more is testament to its ineffectiveness.

Beards and moustaches were common with players, as were full-time jobs. That last point necessitated training sessions at night – usually Tuesday and Wednesday evenings – where the nightly news sports report would include a live cross to one team's session (guaranteed one player would be running around in Speedos and a t-shirt. Why? Beats me).

The finals were still played at the Sydney Cricket Ground even though it was incredibly unsuited to rugby league. The playing surface was in the middle, putting the crowd 15 to 20 metres away from the action. All that empty space made it nigh-on impossible to work out where the sidelines were; it's actually surprising more kickers didn't put the ball out on the full. Cigarette advertising was allowed and the idea of jersey sponsors was new; so new that finalists Cronulla and Canterbury still didn't have one, and Wests had only picked up Victa mid-season.

After the 1977 grand final ended in a draw, prompting extra time, the league changed things up – the next time points were level at full-time in the decider, everyone would be back next weekend for a replay.

No doubt they thought it was unlikely another grand final would end in a draw. And it certainly couldn't possibly happen the very next year. As we will soon see, the big bosses in head office were very wrong on that score. Though it did see the 1978 finals series end on a note of high drama.

1978

The 1978 Season

The 1978 season was marked by a tragedy in Round 10. Prop John Farragher was playing his seventh match for the Panthers, having travelled to the big smoke from the NSW country town of Gilgandra to sign with the Panthers that season. He'd made his debut in Round 4, replacing some guy named Tim Sheens who had been dropped.

Farragher impressed coach Don Parish enough to leave him in the side and the 21-year-old started every match through to Round 10 – which would also be his last game. Playing the Jets at Henson Park, a scrum collapsed, leaving Farragher crumpled on the bottom. A penalty was awarded to the Jets and the players gradually got up off the ground – except for Farragher.

He was rushed to the Royal North Shore Hospital where a few days later, it was confirmed that Farragher had damaged his spinal cord and was a paraplegic. The

"I fell down head-first with the weight behind and on top of me," Farragher said years later on Peter Sterling's TV show *On The Couch*. "I knew I was in trouble straight away. I could tell there was something wrong, it was like the feeling just drained from my feet, and ran all the way up my body."

In the days after the match, Penrith club secretary Ian Maurice watched the footage of the fateful scrum over and over, trying to pin-point what happened. "A scrum was forming and went down with John taking up his position on the blind side," he told the *Sydney Morning Herald*. "He was bent fairly low and the scrum appeared to twist as the players started to push. It twisted to John's left towards the touch line. He was still bent low with his left arm around the Penrith hooker.

"The weight of the scrum appeared to force his head towards his left shoulder. He appeared to lose his balance as the opposition pushed. One of the Newtown players went down on top of John and apparently this is where he suffered his dreadful injury."

Through the year the rugby league world raised money for a fund set up to help Farragher. There was a telethon on Channel 10, teams donated match fees from games against Penrith and the takings from a Cronulla-Monaro Amco Cup match in Canberra were all thrown in. However, some people chose to take advantage; Antonio Samuel Paroli was busted pretending to collect for Farragher when he knocked on the door of a police detective. Paroli ended up in court, where he was sentenced to six months in jail.

The other big story from the 1978 season happened a few weeks after the grand final. Newtown Jets five-eighth Paul Hayward – whose last game for the club was a Round 20 loss to St George – had told his wife he was heading off to the US with his team-mates for the end-of-season trip. Instead, he was flying to Bangkok with drug courier Warren Fellows for a heroin deal. Hayward was there because of his brother-in-law and convicted criminal Neddy Smith. According to Fellows' book, Smith sent Hayward to Bangkok to deliver some money to a friend. With Fellows also heading over, Smith said the two should travel together. "There was absolutely no reason for him to be involved in the events that followed," Fellows said in his book *The Damage Done*.

On the night before they were due to return to Australia, Hayward had gotten paranoid about the suitcase full of heroin in his hotel room. To ease his mind, Fellows had agreed to take charge of the suitcase. But they'd gotten drunk in the player's room and Fellows forgot to take the case with him when he returned to his own room.

The following morning, the police knocked on Fellows' door – they had the suitcase and were demanding he open the combination lock. Inside they found 8.4 kilograms of heroin, packed into 24 bags and hidden under a blue towel. Soon photos of the pair, bound in chains, with the bags of heroin stacked on a table in front of them, were plastered across the Australian papers. Fellows was sentenced to 33 years, while Hayward got 20 years because he was deemed to have been used by the narcotics syndicate.

They served their sentences inside Bang Kwang prison. In a well-known *Rugby League Week* interview published in 1985 Hayward said he was sharing a cell with 26 other men and that he often felt like he was going mad behind bars.

"But when I get really depressed I tell myself, 'don't crack up, you can do it, there's others worse off than you'," he told *RLW* journalist Neil Cadigan. "I think 'God, at least I'm still healthy'. The thing that keeps me going is the hope that one day I'll get out and see my wife and kids again and be able to start all over. I really believe something is going to happen eventually."

Four years after that interview, in April 1989, he was granted a royal pardon as part of the King of Thailand's

1978

60th birthday celebrations. Hayward returned home to Sydney, bringing with him a heroin addiction and HIV picked up by using a contaminated needle while in prison. His life as a free man would be short-lived; struggling to return to normal life, Hayward overdosed on heroin in the bathroom of his family's home in 1992.

On the field, before the start of the 1978 season, defending premiers St George tried to pull a swifty in a trial match at Grafton. They picked a player on the wing named Mickey Lane, who was really known as Mitch Brennan. He was a Brisbane Souths junior but did not have the clearance to play for the Dragons. St George coach Harry Bath didn't bother worrying about that, coaxing him down to trial for the Red V after spotting him in 1975 when coaching at Brisbane Souths.

After signing with the Saints, Brennan tried to blame the mix up on the Grafton ground announcer, who somehow managed to mangle "Mitch Brennan" so badly that it became "Mickey Lane". "Anyway, once they announced me as Mickey Lane we decided to leave it at that to save trouble," Brennan explained. Funnily enough, the Queensland Rugby League weren't buying that for a second, fining him $500 for playing in NSW without the appropriate clearance.

Just two rounds into the 1978 competition, Penrith

hooker Mike Stephenson was getting caned in the scrums by the referees. In the Round 2, ref Jack Danzey threatened to send him off if he kept it up. That prompted Stephenson to switch places with Sheens.

"I have played nearly 400 first grade games and am doing nothing different from when I first started playing," Stephenson said. "I don't know what it is but if I blink I get pinged."

Club officials reckoned they knew what caused the problem; the photo on the front of their annual report. It was an image that showed Stephenson side-on in the tunnel between the two packs – a breach of the rules. "I believe the photo has irked referees," club secretary Maurice said, "and they are getting square with the club by penalising Mike Stephenson for every possible scrum breach." Maurice took the blame, admitting he'd made an error in choosing to put that photo on the cover.

After a Round 3 match against Balmain in which two Canterbury players were concussed Parramatta club doctor Peter Manollaras said players in that situation could be risking brain damage if they played the following week. It was something the league has now only come to terms with in recent years, but Dr Manollaras was talking about standing down concussed players back in 1978.

1978

"I know it sometimes isn't practical for a club to rest a star player for a round because he had concussion, but in normal circumstances nobody should play football in the week after being concussed," Dr Manollaras said.

"However, if a player is concussed two weeks running I have to insist that he be rested for a week. If he is hit again the chances are there that he could suffer permanent brain damage or other serious injury."

Some league fans may recall Sharks star Andrew Ettingshausen suing *GQ* magazine in 1993 for publishing a photo showing him naked in a locker room shower. It wasn't the first time something like that happened. In 1978 Channel 7's Rex Mossop was in the South Sydney sheds doing a few pre-match interviews before the Round 16 clash with Canterbury at Redfern Oval. In footage broadcast on Mossop's *Big League* show, Souths captain Darrell Bampton was seen naked in the background. The balding forward was not happy.

"My wife and children have been ribbed over it," Bampton said. "When I went to work the next day I was greeted with the remark 'what a good show you put on'. I wasn't putting on any show. I was in the room getting changed for a game of football.

"I can't understand why Channel 7 didn't cut the part showing me in the nude."

Bampton got in touch with his lawyers and successfully sued the network for $11,000.

The previous season St George won their first premiership since that golden 11-year run. The players might have celebrated a bit too much in the off season, because the Dragons started 1978 flat, only winning one of their first seven games. Despite clicking for an unbeaten run through rounds eight and 16, they missed the finals by seven points.

"We were still a young side in 1978 and you can lose a bit of focus," Craig Young said. "We probably didn't train as hard as we should have at the start of the year. It's very hard to catch up lost time, especially in rugby league. Then we had some injuries and it didn't work out."

While much of the focus of Round 7 – both at the time and in the years since – was directed at the Wests-Manly match at Lidcombe it wasn't the roughest match that weekend. The grand final rematch between Saints and Parra fit that bill; it just never got the same attention as the Lidcombe match because it wasn't on TV.

In the 1977 rematch, Red Reddy went to town smacking the crap out of the Eels, so they were understandably looking for a little revenge. The *Sydney Morning Herald*'s Alan Clarkson was at Kogarah for the

1978

game. "Tackles were loaded and really meant to hurt," he wrote. "There were punches and two Parramatta players had teeth marks on their stomachs. There were a couple of headbutts and several Parramatta players complained that knuckles had been ground into their eyes."

Three players were given early showers that afternoon (only one player in the Wests-Manly clash was marched). Dragons prop Young went for kneeing, and the Eels' Lew Platz and Ed Sulkowicz were also marched, the latter for hitting Saints No6 Ken Kearney in the face and opening up a wound over his right eye. Young and Platz got four-week suspensions while Sulkowicz got a week. The league also cited and suspended Eel Ron Hilditch for two weeks, while Reddy and Robert Stone – called up over the biting allegations – seemed to have gotten off without any punishment.

Over at Lidcombe that weekend was the match that set the Fibros vs Silvertails legend into stone. The animosity had started in the pre-season, when Wests and Manly went down to Melbourne to take part in the Festival of Football, where an Aussie rules and soccer match would also be played. Even though there was nothing on the line, new coach Roy Masters gave the order to smash the Manly kicker after they put up the ball (the Melbourne refs would watch the flight of the ball and ignore what was going on in back play). By the end of the meaningless match both Manly and Wests ended up with players in the casualty ward.

In Round 7, Masters had his players wound to fever pitch, smashing the lockers in the change room and calling out which Manly players they were going to hit. It was unleashed in just the second tackle of the match, when Wests John Donnelly launched a swinging arm at the head of Terry Randall. From there it was on, all screened into people's lounge rooms as it was the TV match of the round.

Unhappy about the look, the league cited both Donnelly and Les Boyd – neither of whom had been sent off during the match (the only player to go was Manly's Stephen Knight for a coat hanger tackle late in the match). Donnelly got three weeks and Boyd copped four.

Donnelly wore it, Boyd didn't. He took the league to court – in part because he wasn't allowed to call witnesses – and won. The league decided to retry Boyd, let him call those witnesses and suspended him for four weeks anyway.

The potential for violence continued in the days after the Round 7 fixtures, with referees Gary Cook and

1978

Dennis Braybrook receiving death threats. Midway through the Dragons-Eels match a man called 2UE radio to utter the message "Cook is a dead man". Two days later there was a second call at home. "I was out but my wife took the call," Cook told *Rugby League Week*. "I have since asked the local police to watch my home." Braybrook was forced to get a silent telephone number following a few death threats after the Wests-Manly clash.

Despite it being a bit of a fizzer in the 1977 season, the League-A-Thon – a precursor to Magic Round – took place. All the matches were played at the Sydney Cricket Ground; three on Sunday and another three on the Anzac Day Tuesday. With tickets just $2, they pulled in a crowd of 44,507 on the Sunday but complaints about long queues and insufficient toilet facilities filtered out and the Anzac Day crowd dropped to 25,004.

The season saw the oddity of the Rugby League Olympics at Leichhardt Oval in early April. Players competed in Olympic-style events, including running, arm wrestling, tug of war and a 13-man shuttle relay. Manly ended up in top spot overall, earning a big novelty cheque worth $10,000.

At the Olympics, first-year Balmain star Larry Corowa (who had requested the media stop calling him the "Black Flash" as he found it offensive) became the fastest man in league by winning the 100-metre sprint. He left a five-metre gap between himself and second-placed Russel Gartner.

In September he showed his speed credentials again, defeating Stawell Gift winner Steve Proudlock over 100 metres at Wentworth Park. Corowa put that speed to good use on the field, becoming the season's top tryscorer with 24 – which accounted for 20 per cent of the Tigers' points that year. That honour saw him pocket $1000 from Hutton's Footy Franks, with Corowa pledging to put it in the bank while he worked out how to spend it.

In second spot on the tryscorer list – and a long way back – was Mick Cronin with 16 tries. Though the Parramatta centre could console himself with the fact that his 117 goals gave him a combined points total of 282 – the biggest in the 1978 season. Winning the Rothmans Medal for the second year running couldn't have hurt either.

Despite having a shot at making the finals right up to the last round, Easts officials were furious that Channel 7 did not televise a single one of their games. The only other teams to be ignored were Newtown and Norths – who finished last and second-last. Being lumped in with those two sides seemed to infuriate the Roosters even more. "I could understand the channel's attitude if we were one of the also-rans," secretary manager Ron Jones said. "But we have a chance of making the final five and some of our players are in the superstar bracket."

Jones then made the foolish complaint that he'd expected Channel 7 should have screened their last-round game against Manly rather than opting for the Sharks-Wests match. Given the latter game would decide the minor premiership, it was no surprise Channel 7 pointed their cameras that way.

That Easts-Manly match was the last one for lock forward Ron Coote, who decided to hang up the boots after 257 matches. Coote had started out with Souths in 1964, playing for the Bunnies for eight seasons and being part of their grand final wins in 1967-68 and 1970-71. Coote then switched to the Roosters for the 1972 season, winning two more premierships in 1974-75. During a 15-season career he played 24 Test matches in an Australian jumper and a further 10 in the World Cup.

Coote said he would have retired after the 1976 season but played on because he wanted to help out new coach Arthur Beetson. Winning the Harry Sunderland Medal in two Test series against England was his career highlight. "But playing in six winning grand final sides also ranks pretty highly, as does the time when I captained the World Cup team to victory," he said.

"I played in nine grand finals, including one against St George, which drew a rugby league record crowd of 78,000 to the SCG."

The 1978 Combatants

Western Suburbs Magpies

Thanks in part to the "Fibros vs Silvertails" legend and Wests' familiarity with the bottom of the ladder during their final seasons as a standalone club, there is a lingering image of the Western Suburbs Magpies as a team of battlers. While those Silvertails – aka Manly-Warringah – were cashed-up and buying premierships.

So it can be hard to get your head around the fact that Western Suburbs was once known as The Millionaires, looking to splash out the cash as a way to win the comp. In 1952, they won their last premiership, then somehow managed to end up with the wooden spoon 12 months later. The fall from grace was so comprehensive that they spent the last eight weeks of the comp in last place. The only team they beat in those eight weeks? Manly, funnily enough.

By the mid-1950s Wests officials decided to buy their way up the ladder. While other clubs complained Wests

1978

were driving up the price of players, the tactic worked. They made the finals every year from 1956 to 1963, playing in the grand final in 1958 and three years in a row from 1961-63. The only thing in the way of premiership glory was a rampaging St George side, who beat Wests in each of those deciders, while raking up 11 straight titles.

And then the money must have run out for the Millionaires for they didn't play finals footy for more than a decade. In 1974, Wests snuck into the finals in fifth spot and then beat Souths and Manly before coming up against the Roosters in the final. The black and whites got rolled 25-2; which was not unexpected. Easts had only lost three games all season and won the minor premiership by eight points.

The only glory the Magpies had in that dry spell was winning the 1977 Amco Cup – over Easts coincidentally – though with the side running down the bottom of the ladder in the weekend comp, there was talk the club had forgotten about the regular season to focus on the midweek competition and the cash prize it offered. There is some support for that argument; either side of the Amco Cup semi they were walloped – 47-10 by the Sharks and 40-0 by the Bears. And the weekend following the cup win, Saints rolled over them 49-4. Still, when your trophy cabinet has been bare for so long, any piece of silverware is worth going for.

The 1978 season was shaping up as something special for long-suffering Magpies fans. Roy Masters had signed on as coach and sparked a massive turnaround in form. In 1977, they'd finished ninth with just seven wins, scoring 247 points but leaking 438. But by the end of the 1978 regular season, they were minor premiers for the first time since 1961, winning 16 matches, and lifting their pointscoring by almost 200 to 426. At the same time they stiffened their defence, limiting the season's opponents to 288 points. While there is the aura of the biff that surrounds the 1978 Magpies – and not without some justification – it was their pointscoring that saw them finish as minor premiers. A crucial component was goalkicker and former Wallaby Peter Rowles, who finally cemented his place in the No6 jersey for 1978. He scored 229 – more than half – of Wests points that season. It was only a record-breaking 260 points from the Eels' Mick Cronin on the way to his second Rothmans Medal that stopped Rowles from being the competition's leading pointscorer. The pair were far ahead of the pack; the third best pointscorer was the Sharks' Barry Andrews almost 100 points further back.

1978

Masters said the biff was a contributor to his team's high points tally. "Part of our tactics was to stir the opposition up for the first 20 minutes," Masters revealed. "They would look for revenge and while they were looking for it we'd spend the next 60 minutes playing with skill."

Though the biff does make for some great stories. Among those are tussles with Manly, one of which occurred during a pre-season "festival of football" in Melbourne, which was the start of the Fibros-Silvertails legend. Masters noted the referees were Melbourne-based and so were looking at the flight of the ball rather than the players. "I told them to whack them in back play, to give them a tickle up every time they kicked the ball," Masters said.

While that pre-season exhibition match set the tone for both the Magpies' season and the Fibros vs Silvertails legend, what gets overlooked is that the tactic didn't work – Manly won that game in Melbourne 12-5. And when the Magpies went to Brookvale late in the season, they were defeated again.

It was television that ensured the Fibros and Silvertails would live long in the memory of league fans. That Round 7 clash at Lidcombe – which Wests did in fact win – was televised, bringing the biff into people's lounge room on the Sunday replay and then living on forever via video cassettes, DVD and YouTube. The rivalry worked against the Magpies; the league hated the black eye those images gave the game and so began a slow process of cracking down on the rough stuff. Despite Wests' reputation, not one of their players was sent off in the 1978; several players were later cited and suspended but none were actually marched by the referee.

During the season, captain Tom Raudonikis told *Rugby League Week* Masters was the reason for the team's boost in form; he had them playing like "starving dogs". "Roy knows where the fine line is and he takes it just that far," Raudonikis said. "You wouldn't believe how fired up we get before a game – and it happens every week, which is why our defence is so keen."

If there was a question mark hanging over the Magpies' title quest, it was their away record. While they were undefeated at Lidcombe with an 11-0 record, when they travelled they were a much less impressive 5-5 (with one draw). And none of the finals matches would be played in the western suburbs.

1978

Cronulla Sharks

Of the teams in the top five, the Cronulla-Sutherland Sharks were the youngest, having only joined the league just over a decade earlier in 1967. In that first season, they signed a host of players with first-grade experience, and as coach landed Ken Kearney, who had been part of six of the St George Dragons 11 straight premierships. The Sharks won their first match, beating Easts at the Sydney Sports Ground, but could only manage two more victories to finish with the wooden spoon.

The following year they doubled the number of wins, finishing 10th on the ladder out of 12 teams. The bright spots in that year included moving to Endeavour Field and half Terry Hughes beating future immortal Johnny Raper by a point to take out the inaugural Rothmans Medal. They went back down to the cellar in 1969 but had a stroke of good fortune in landing British international Tommy Bishop. In a bizarre set of circumstances, Bishop had flown to Australia without signing to a club; Easts had shown interest but had backed out by the time his plane landed at Mascot. Stuck halfway around the world with no team to play for, Cronulla was the only other club that wanted him. Though he wasn't exactly pleased with the situation. "They'd only just come into the competition and I thought, 'bloody hell, I've gone from the captain of England and St Helens to the worst team in Australia," he said.

They didn't stay that way for long. When Kearney left at the end of the 1969 season, Bishop took over as captain-coach. For the next few seasons they hung around the middle of the ladder until 1973 came along. The Sharks had a massive form improvement, finishing second on the ladder only a point behind minor premiers Manly.

In the finals, the Sharks blotted big brother the Dragons 18-0 before losing to Manly 14-4 in the major semi. A 20-11 win over Newtown in the final set up a rematch in the grand final with the Sea Eagles in what has gone down as the most brutal rugby league decider ever (though TV wasn't around before to catch whatever happened in most of the earlier grand finals).

1978

"Every illegality was used in those 40 minutes of the first half," the *Sydney Morning Herald* reported, "and several times play exploded into a brawling mass of players. In one explosion about 20 players were involved at various parts of the field with a dozen milling around one spot. Every tackle in those hectic minutes was loaded with menace and was meant to damage. There were punches, kneeing and kicking as the rough play raged from one end of the field to the other."

Yet, surprisingly referee Keith Page didn't send off a single player. The main difference between the two sides was Bob Fulton, who scored a try in both halves and looked to be running at a different speed to everyone else. When the final siren sounded, the Sharks had lost 10-7, prompting Bishop's English team-mate Cliff Watson to say they should have whacked Fulton and forced him off rather than dishing that punishment to forward Malcolm Reilly.

Bishop was being robbed of coach of the year honours that. Despite taking the Sharks from eight wins in 1972 to 17, he lost to Newtown's Jack Gibson, who improved the Bluebags' record by just three wins, from 11 to 14.

If Sharks fans thought 1973 would herald a run of finals appearances and maybe a premiership in the coming years, they were very much mistaken. Between 1974 and 1977, Cronulla didn't play finals footy; not even having Johnny Raper as coach for 1976-77 helped matters. But another Dragon did; Norm Provan signed on as coach for the 1978 season, which saw the club finish second on the ladder. They kicked off the season with a seven-match winning streak – eight if you could the 57-5 Amco Cup shellacking of Newcastle. Also, later in the season they put together a five-match streak.

However, in what may have been a bad omen, the Sharks lost both of their home and away matches against Manly.

1978

Manly-Warringah Sea Eagles

For Manly, the 1978 season was a time to put a firm lock on their claim as the team of the 1970s. They'd already won three premierships – in '72, '73 and '76 – so a fourth in 1978 would seal it. The decade was the Sea Eagles feast after a long, long period of famine. One that stretched all the way back to their inception in 1947.

The first time they made it to the big dance – when they were still known by the less threatening name of the Seagulls – was in 1951 just four years after their birth. It was only a weird quirk of the rules at the time that deprived them of the premiership. Back then if the minor premiers were defeated in the finals they had the right to challenge whoever won the final. Any other year, the final was the match that decided the premiers. But not in 1951, where Manly beat St George in the final.

The Dragons had knocked minor premiers Souths out of the finals with a 35-8 flogging, suggesting the Bunnies didn't deserve a second chance. But, after the Manly final win, the Bunnies came in and said 'I challenge you!". So Manly had to play them, and got smashed 42-14.

Their next pair of appearances, in 1957 and 1959, were cases of very bad timing for those GFs were won by the Dragons during their 11-straight streak. In the 1968 and 1970 decider, they came up against another juggernaut in the Rabbitohs, who were in the midst of their run of four premierships in five years. That 1970 decider is best remembered for Manly's John Bucknall smashing John Sattler's jaw early in the game; which history showed accomplished little but putting Bucknall in his own world of pain as Satts' team-mates all took their retribution in every tackle.

In 1971, the side finished minor premiers for the first time in its history, but lost to Souths and then St George to miss the grand final (that stupid "minor premiers can challenge" rule had been well and truly turfed by this time). The Manly side might not have won the big one coming into the 1970s, but something was building. And it didn't hurt that the club weakened main rival Souths by buying a few of their stars ahead of the 1972 season in Ray Branighan and John O'Neill. Those signings helped created enmity among the ranks of South supporters and other clubs for what was seen as poaching by Manly, though Branighan later said that was incorrect; it was he who approached Manly about signing up because he was unhappy with what Souths was offering.

"Souths thought they owned you," Branighan told author Alan Whiticker. "If you were a junior, they thought that it was their God-given right to offer you nothing and expect you to stay".

While playing for Australia in the 1970 World Cup, Branighan said Ken Arthurson told him to call if he ever had any problems. So at the end of the '71 season he called and Arko offered him money to come over. "I wasn't on big money at Manly but I stayed with the club because they looked after me and my family," Branighan said.

Star Manly player Bob Fulton knew those Souths signings – and the others who took advantage of the Sea Eagles' chequebook – would make a difference. "We had the brilliance to win games but we didn't have the steel. We became very strong with the influx of these players."

Those signings pushed the Sea Eagles to the next level; again finishing minor premiers in 1972, they were able to go all the way and win their first premiership with a 19-14 victory over Easts. A second followed in 1973, their chance of a hat-trick taken away by a minor semi loss to Wests in 1974.

The Manly side were stopped in the final in 1975 by Easts (who entered the finals on a 19-match winning streak, finishing the regular season on top an astonishing 10 points ahead of second place) but chalked up their third premiership of the 1970s the following season over a Parramatta team playing its first grand final.

There was a slump of sorts in 1977, the club losing eight games – the most in a single season in the 1970s to date and just squeaking into the finals in fifth spot. Part of that could be put down to the loss of Bob Fulton, who went to Easts – the poacher had turned into the poached. Late in the 1978 season, the Sea Eagles were at risk of missing the finals altogether; three straight losses in rounds 15-17 saw them drop out of the five. They managed to right the ship, winning their last five matches of the regular season, which included a 26-4 win over the No1 team in Cronulla. The Manly side entered the finals with momentum and a chance to continue their dominance of the 1970s. But what would transpire in the finals would mean they'd have a hard road to go all the way.

1978

Canterbury Bankstown Bulldogs

Things didn't start well for Canterbury-Bankstown. Allowed into the league in 1935, they were the whipping boys of the competition and the subject of much derision. "Whoever told the hyphenates they could play football is the world's greatest legpuller," the *Truth* newspaper wrote in that first season. "But the joke's on rugby league for accepting a combination that would be towelled by a team of salmon-tin dribblers. And they're fixing to up a brand-new ground for them. What for? To use for kiss-in-the-ring, or just to gambol about like lambs in the spring?"

The team only won twice that season – both against the even more hopeless University side who was two years away from giving it all up. That first season saw

Canterbury on the wrong end of what is still the biggest losing margin in league history.

In Round 5 the Dragons annihilated them 91-6 in what may well be the only match in league history where every player on the winning team scored points. It's possible the fact that two of the three footballs used were made of rubber may have inflated the scoreline – it probably would have helped the goalkicker Les Griffin land 15 conversions.

You'd think an 85-point margin would be hard to beat; but Easts came close the following week in an 87-7 whipping, meaning Canterbury racked up the two biggest defeats in history in successive weeks. The club proved to be fast learners; a year later they made the semis and in 1938 finished top of the ladder and went on to win the comp. They would win it all again in 1942 and then came decades without premiership glory. In that time they made just two grand finals, losing in 1967 to Souths; though that season saw them end the Dragons' legendary premiership run by defeating them in the final.

The other decider was in 1974, where they lost to Easts. There were signs in the 1970s that Canterbury was building to something, making the finals in five of the seasons going into 1978. It was the first featuring all three of the Hughes and the Mortimer brothers; Chris Mortimer had been the last of the six to sign up. And footballing doctor George Peponis would break through for Australian selection in 1978. The 1978 season also saw the club jettison their old nickname of the Berries, which obviously didn't lend itself to a mascot costume that wouldn't look stupid. The club put forward some alternatives to the supporters and the Bulldog was the resounding winner. Working against the club in 1978 was a run of injuries – half/five-eighth Tim Pickup was the only player to take the field in every game. In 1978, they had the chance to finish much higher than fifth; two draws against Penrith cost them, as did a poor performance in a 15-2 loss to the Tigers. "Balmain did not play well enough to deserve to win and our loss was a real heartbreak," coach Ted Glossop said.

However, for the fans, it felt as though a victorious season might be just around the corner.

Parramatta Eels

Since their team came into the competition in 1947 it had been hard to be an Eels fan. They'd been waiting all that time for the team's first premiership and in that time had experienced many more troughs than peaks. Things weren't great right from their first season; it took the Eels until the ninth round to record their first competition win and then they ended 1947 with the wooden spoon – a dubious honour with which they would become quite familiar.

The 1950s were especially dire for the new team, finishing last six times, and six times in a row from 1956 to 1961. But then the sun shone in the 1962 season when Dragons legend Ken Kearney took over as coach. After winning just three games the year before, the Eels won nine of 18 matches (along with a pair of draws) and landed in the finals for the first time. They'd made the post-season at a time when St George and Wests were strong, and so didn't make much headway, but the turnaround in form was impressive nonetheless. That upward trajectory continued for the three years of Killer Kearney's coaching, culminating in a second-place finish in 1964, just two points behind a Dragons side on the way to their ninth premiership. In the major semi the St George side humbled Parramatta 42-0.

The doldrums set in again for the most of the remaining decade, with the Eels only making the finals once following Kearney's departure. They reacquainted themselves with the wooden spoon in 1970, winning just four matches all year. Another of those stunning reversals of form came with 1971, the Parramatta side landing in the finals with 12 wins, though the Saints bundled them out in the first week.

The following season it was back down to the cellar for Parramatta. There would be no more finals for the Eels until 1975. That season they were in a three-way tie with Balmain and Wests for the fifth spot. After winning their last-round match on the Sunday, the Eels had to play Wests on Tuesday and Balmain on Thursday, defeating both to make the finals. Despite having played three matches that week already, the Eels managed to defeat Canterbury 6-5 that weekend.

The 1976 season saw the spark of hope beginning to burn. New coach Terry Fearnley took over and he brought Easts' John Peard over to the Eels and introduced the bomb as an attacking option in the opponents' quarter. And it was the same year a future legend of the club in Ray Price first took the field for the Eels.

That season they finished second and knocked over St George and then Manly to make it to their first grand final, a rematch with the Sea Eagles. The club scorned the football gods by foolishly holding a street parade to celebrate their grand final debut. That was obviously tempting fate and so the gods responded with some heartbreak for the Eels. Behind 11-10 Eels centre John Moran passed to winger Neville Glover 10 metres from the line with no defender to beat. The pass was high on his shoulder – Glover later said he overran the pass – and he dropped it. And with it went the hopes of Eels fans.

The following year the footballing gods showed they weren't quite done with the Eels. That was Mick Cronin's first year with the club, having to break a verbal agreement with the Bulldogs to sign with the Eels (it's hard to imagine these days, but Cronin had already

1978

represented Australia by then, picked while still playing for Gerringong).

The club landed its first minor premiership and fans figured the experience of 1976 would stand them in good stead. The Eels lost to the Dragons 10-5 in the major semi before making their way to the grand final with a 13-5 win over Easts. There was no street parade this time, but the footy gods created more heartbreak late in the match. A try to Eels centre Ed Sulkowicz near the corner levelled the score at 11-all, with Cronin needed to convert to give Parra their first title. He sprayed the kick to the right – Cronin had been having kicking issues throughout the finals, landing one from four in the major semi and two from eight in the prelim final. Extra time didn't change the score so both sides had to return the following weekend for a rematch. The Dragons dished out some rough stuff on the way to a 22-0 win; Fearnley copping criticism from his players for not allowing them to retaliate.

The 1978 season saw the Eels a little shaky. After winning their first two matches, they lost five of their next six games to put them in eighth spot on the ladder. They managed to turn things around and won eight of their next nine matches. Still, it wasn't until the last round that their place in the finals was assured. The club's up and down season left people wondering whether the Eels were heading for another one of those all-too-familiar troughs.

1978

The Last Round

1 Wests (15-5-1)………….. 31 points
2 Cronulla (15-6)…………. 30 points
3 Manly (14-7)……………. 28 points
4 Canterbury (13-7-1)……. 27 points
5 Parramatta (13-8)………. 26 points

———

6 Easts (13-8)…………….. 26 points

The last round was of the sort rugby league bosses dream about. The top five was still not settled, all spots still up for grabs. Easts were just out of the top five, Parramatta just in. Either could make the finals depending on the result of their final round match. The Eels had an easier final match-up against the last-placed Jets. Easts, on the other hand, would have to overcome Manly to push their way into the post-season. If both sides won, and Canterbury lost their last-round fixture, then the Dogs would drop out of the five.

To make things more interesting, there was the possibility that midweek playoffs may be required to sort things out. This was back in the day when the league didn't bother to use points differential to work out where everyone finished. Footy bible *Rugby League Week* thought that a stupid way to run things. "What would happen if six teams tied for fourth?" *RLW*'s Geoff Prenter wrote ahead of the last round. "There would be play-offs until Christmas."

By the way, if you're not a fan of the permutations of a rugby league table, feel free to skip ahead a few paragraphs. In 1978, for-and-against didn't matter, playoffs were how decisions were made when it got to the pointy end. Which meant going into the final round, there was a chance for a three-way tie. If Easts and Parramatta both won, they'd be level with Manly on 28 points – requiring two midweek matches. There was even the outside chance of having *four* teams tied on 28 points after the final round, which would have had some stats geeks salivating. That would see three knockout matches played between the Sunday of the last round and the Saturday of the first semi. Granted, that scenario depended on Canterbury playing out a draw with second-last Penrith – a highly unlikely occurrence. And

1978

yet Canterbury managed it with a 7-7 full-time score after leading 7-0 at half-time.

The Eels ran in 14 tries to wallop the Jets 62-18 (that was in the three-point try era. In today's money, the Eels scored 76 points). Though *Rugby League Week* didn't think the Eels' win over the Jets was a big deal. "Beating Newtown these days is as easy as stealing a lollypop from the hands of a baby," the paper claimed.

Despite a finals place to play for, Easts got done by Manly 20-10, with Sea Eagles captain Terry Randall leading the way with his physical defence. It was good enough for him to score a 9/10 in the much-vaunted *RLW* player ratings.

Manly crowed about how the premiership was already theirs. "This side has got as good a chance as any we've had of winning the premiership," boss Ken Arthurson said. "We've got the best team in the competition and we'll win it."

Easts coach Arthur Beetson criticised Greg Hartley for the way he refereed the match. "We were penalised heavily early and he wasn't consistent," Big Artie said. "If you penalise our players for not getting off the man when tackled, you should penalise the other side for it too. He didn't."

Another factor working against Easts was that they

may not have been at their best due to playing the Amco Cup final just five days earlier – this was back in the day when the bright sparks in rugby league HQ figured it was a brilliant idea to have the mid-week comp wrap up just days before the finals. It wouldn't be until 1985 that the Wednesday night fixtures would end a full month before the finals.

Easts beat St George 16-4 in the mid-week game where fresh allegations of some Dragons players going the chomp surfaced. In the second quarter, Easts fullback Russell Fairfax held up his middle finger to referee Jack Danzey to show the bite marks. Captain Bob Fulton spoke up after the match, claiming half his team was bitten. "A few times St George players attempted to bite me," he said. "I was able to pull my arm and hand away in time for them not to get their teeth into me."

As expected, Saints officials refuted the allegations – which had also been made earlier this season by other teams. "If we hear of any further allegations we will take the people responsible to court," club secretary John Fleming said. "We are not going to sit back any longer and have our name dragged through the mud."

So, at the end of the last round, Manly stayed where they were on the ladder, while Parramatta and

1978

Canterbury swapped places and the Roosters went costume-shopping for Mad Monday.

Despite the threat of congestion at the lower end of the five, the big game was up at the top. In a piece of good fortune, the two candidates for the minor premiership – the Magpies and the Sharks – met at Endeavour Field in the last round, with first place on the line. And, as expected, it was a physical affair.

Sharks hooker John McMartin would say after the match he was punched in the first scrum by three separate Wests players. "Punches came from everywhere," McMartin said, "and I knew Wests were after me." The Sharks matched it in the physicality stakes, in fact going a bit overboard. In the eighth minute there was a moment that would have a huge bearing on the Sharks' finals chances. Referee Jack Danzey gave scary prop Dane Sorenson his marching orders after he hit Wests hardman Les Boyd with an elbow. His teammate Steve Kneen could consider himself very lucky not to be joining him on the sideline after clocking decoy runner Geoff Foster on the very same play.

The dramas around the Sorenson send-off and the Kneen oversight would play out in the week leading up to the first round of the finals.

Despite playing a man down for almost the entire

match, the Sharks took a 10-5 lead into half-time. Thanks to Wests' ill-discipline, Steve Rogers had five penalty shots and landed them all – including one from almost halfway. Three minutes from the break, Graeme O'Grady scored off a scrum near the Sharks' line to add to a Peter Rowles' penalty shot that had opened the scoring.

In the second half, the Sharks continued to play like a team with a full complement of 13 players, finding gaps in the Wests' line. They were close to going further in front when half Steve Hansard scooted through the Magpies defence on halfway, before flinging it to Rogers who threw a looping pass to winger Steve Edmonds, who quickly offloaded to Paul Khan on the inside. His pass went to ground less than a metre from the Wests line, Greg Pierce bombing a gift three-pointer by knocking on as he tried to pick it up.

In the 52nd minute Sharks fullback Mick Mullane scored an embarrassingly easy try. Fifteen metres out, he was at dummy half and took advantage of the skinniest of blind sides and skated along the sideline untouched to score. Rogers converted to make it 15-7 and the minor premiership looked like it might be going to the shire.

That try must have woken up the Magpies. Over the next seven minutes they put on 10 points from tries to

1978

Boyd and Don Moseley and two goals to Rowles to take the lead 17-15 with 15 minutes to go. Rogers kicked a penalty goal from right in front to level it up with 13 minutes left on the clock. Rogers sprayed a field goal attempt but a few minutes later, in the 74th minute, Rowles landed one after a long break from fullback John Dorahy gave the Magpies field position. That one-point lead was enough for the Magpies to win their first minor premiership since 1961 and their fifth overall.

<u>Major Preliminary Semi-Final</u>

Cronulla Sharks vs Manly Sea Eagles
Sydney Cricket Ground
Saturday, August 26

In the lead-up to the first weekend of the finals all the attention was on the Sorenson send-off in the Sharks-Wests match, as well as the fact Kneen somehow stayed on the field. How referee Jack Danzey and his sideline officials missed Kneen jumping up to clock decoy runner Foster across the jaw with an elbow on the very same play as the Sorenson hit on Boyd was a headscratcher; they literally happened side-by-side. They were close enough for the Channel 7 camera situated behind the goalposts to easily fit both Sorenson's and

1978

Kneen's actions into the one frame.

Wests' Roy Masters was surprised the Sharks came out with the physical stuff right from the kick-off - perhaps because that was Wests' thing. "I didn't think Cronulla played that sort of football," he said after the match.

In a gobsmacking move, referees boss Eric Cox cleared Danzey and touch judges Max Tomsett and Jack Farrelly. He said neither touchie could be blamed for missing Kneen's hit on Foster. "I was at the game and saw the incident involving Dane Sorenson but missed the other one," Cox said. "There were arms and legs flying everywhere and nobody can blame either touch judge for not reporting the other incident."

Then Cox made himself look a little more foolish by issuing an edict that foul play would not be tolerated in the finals – that would be the same sort of foul play his officials had just missed.

"If you think it's going to be like past years you can forget about it," he said. "There won't be any illegal softening-up period and no foul play at all.

"I'm reminding players now and I've reminded my referees. Players tried it last Sunday at Endeavour and it didn't come off."

Except that, as far as Kneen was concerned, it *did*

come off. League HQ didn't help matters by declining to use the video footage that Channel 7 viewers had seen on Sunday night to cite Kneen. "Incidents like the one on Sunday are in the hands of the referee and touch judges," NSW Rugby League President Kevin Humphreys said. This was despite the league willingly using TV footage to cite several players after that now-legendary Wests-Manly match at Lidcombe earlier in the season.

The Sun justifiably criticised the league's inaction on a transgression that had been replayed on TV news for days after the match, saying it was a "head in the sand attitude".

"TV film was used in suspending three players earlier and it is continually called by players appearing before the judiciary," the paper reported on the back page. "But in a remarkable statement, Kevin Humphreys said he was strongly opposed to citing players over individual incidents."

Wests officials were fuming that Kneen looked to be home free and planned to cite him. "We feel pretty strongly about the whole thing," said Wests secretary Gary Russell. "We had two players cited earlier in the year and they got a total of seven weeks' suspension. Citing the player, we believe, is the only right course to take."

Well, unless the other side threatens to dob in one of your players. Cronulla secretary Arthur Winn publicly warned Wests not to go and open that Pandora's box. "We might take the whole film down to the judiciary and go through all players," he said.

"We could have a parade. I think they'll find there are a few more incidents that the judiciary might like to see." The rumour was that Cronulla had spotted a key Magpies player kicking an opponent, as well as several others punching in scrums.

The threat has the desired effect; Wests backed down, much to the chagrin of Foster who had been left with a bruised jaw and five stitches. The second rower's face was so swollen that his employer – the NSW Police Force – told him to take the week off work. He wasn't impressed with his club's decision to let sleeping dogs lie.

He was concussed by the incident and, though he played on, had no memory of the match. "I was in a complete blackout. It's an eerie feeling – I can't even remember what coach Roy Masters said at half-time."

Foster's solicitor had advised him to take Kneen to court but Foster declined, not wanting to seem like "a big sheila".

Kneen knew full well he had just dodged a bullet. "I have to be lucky I haven't been called in by the league," he said. "My club hasn't instructed me about speaking of the incident, but I don't want to say anything."

As for Sorenson, the Sharks were hoping to use the defence of mistaken identity, claiming the referee saw Foster on the ground and then blamed the Sharks prop. It didn't work, nor did the surprising step of Boyd appearing at the judiciary to support Sorenson. A four-week suspension was handed out, meaning the hardman would miss the entire finals series. Cronulla president Steve Hodsdon said they hadn't given up hope of a last-minute-reprieve.

"I've seen the film shown during the judiciary hearing and I don't feel it is conclusive," he said. "We are desperate to find something that will clear Dane. I'll be talking with Cronulla officials today to see how many television stations took film of the match."

Try as they might, the Sharks could find no footage that would give Sorenson a get of jail free card. If they were going to win their first premiership in 1978, it would be without the New Zealander. "I'm bitterly disappointed I can't play in the grand final if Cronulla makes it but my absence will just make the rest of the team try that much harder," Sorenson said.

1978

The unenviable job of stepping into the huge hole left by Sorensen for the finals match against Manly fell on the inexperienced shoulders of Gary Stares, who had only played four matches that season. And two of those had him on the bench.

Even with Sorenson in the side, the Sharks hadn't been able to beat Manly all season; it wasn't even close, Cronulla lost 27-8 and 26-4 (and there was also a 36-15 loss in the Craven Mild Cup pre-season tournament).

The Sharks were never going to be favourites in the major preliminary semi, but the absence of Sorenson saw the bookies put a big red line through them – Manly were 2/1 favourites to win on Saturday. This was despite them going into the game without half/five-eighth Steve Martin and forward John Harvey, the latter of whom had played virtually every weekend in 1978.

One crucial player Manly would have at their disposal was Terry Randall – who had started his career as a centre before the Sea Eagles' 1973 coach Ron Willey figured the guy would go better in the forwards. Suspended for four weeks after delivering a head-high tackle in a Round 15 clash to Canterbury, the break did Randall good. He'd been able to overcome a series of injuries and returned in Round 20 full of fire.

"That suspension may have come as a blessing in disguise," said coach Frank Stanton. "It's great to have him firing so well at semi-final time. He can take charge of a game almost on his own and that's the kind of man you need to go on with it."

The media were setting themselves up for a battle between Randall and Steve Kneen, who were rivals for the second row in the Kangaroo squad at the end of the year. But the player Stanton had the most time for was Alan Thompson; he said he picked the five-eighth first and then built the rest of the team around him. "Next to Fulton he has the best football brain in the game," the coach said. "He is fundamentally tops in all aspects of the game. A perfect passer of the ball, he is above all a team player. Add a neat step and adequate pace plus the ability to play lock, halfback, centre, five-eighth, wing and fullback and you come up with one out of the box."

Over at the Sharks, coach Norm Provan seemed to have changed his mind again about his key playmaker. He'd given Barry Andrews the No6 jersey for the first half of the season, before handing it over to Martin Raftery in Round 13. The medical student held onto the position right through to the eve of the finals, when Provan went back to Andrews (the whole time they had high-priced Balmain recruit Greg Cox struggling to get a

1978

game at all, spending the season playing in the halves in reserve grade). The swap came at the last minute, just two days before the match; if it was designed as a curveball to mess with Stanton's plans, then it worked.

Raftery was in the Sharks line-up for all three Manly matches and studying film through the week led to Stanton spotting a weakness in Raftery – which immediately became useless when Provan switched things up.

In the day before the match, *The Sun* posted an obviously ghostwritten column from Manly fullback Graham Eadie. It's a sure bet that not once in his life had Eadie said his pack would "eat" the opposition. Nor would a seasoned player be so foolish as to tempt fate by saying "grand final here we come". Eadie – or whoever wrote the piece – felt Manly's biggest foe was complacency.

"Three big wins in three games against Cronulla could be our worst enemy," the column said. "Frank Stanton will knock that out of us before kick-off time, and the match will become one of three grand finals we have to win to become premiers."

Steve Rogers also had a ghostwriter, who felt silencing Johnny Gibbs would be the key to victory. "Gibbs is the danger man. He is a great attacker if given latitude. If we can minimise his breaks we will come up with enough tries to win."

In the first half, coming up with even one try seemed beyond the Sharks. In the ninth minute, centre Dave Chamberlin gapped them and had fullback Mick Mullane in support, but Mullane was ruled offside with the line wide open. A few minutes later, Chamberlain broke through again with Mullane in support only to throw the pass forward. The pair managed to cut through the right-side Manly defence easily, but just couldn't convert those breaks into points.

Fortunately for the Cronulla side, Manly were having just as much trouble finding any points at all. It wasn't until the 24th minute that Gibbs broke the 0-0 deadlock with the strangest of options – a field goal. "I thought if we had a point start it would lift our game," he explained after the match. It was an odd decision, Thompson had broken through the Sharks defence to get five metres from the line. Though it was now the last tackle; rather than put up a bomb and hope to jag a try, Gibbs potted the field goal for a 1-0 lead.

What was more unusual is that Gibbs had another go a few minutes later. This time the kick went into the right upright, after which time Gibbs decided that was enough field goal shots for one match.

1978

At any rate, the 1-0 scoreline didn't lift the Manly side like Gibbs had hoped. The score stayed unchanged until just before half-time, when Gibbs got the ball in his hands. Just outside the Manly quarter, he was too far away for another shot at goal. Instead, he jogged across field before popping a sublime pass to centre Russel Gartner that put him straight through a gap. Crossing halfway, he put on a bodyswerve to beat Mullane before offloading to Tom Mooney.

With the Sharks cover defence now swarming, Mooney lobbed the ball back to Gartner to score in the corner. Eadie missed the sideline conversion and Manly went into the sheds up 4-0.

That was a scoreline that seriously flattered the Sea Eagles, and they must have surely realised it. It was only by the grace of the footy gods that Manly wasn't behind by double digits. The Sharks had bombed at least three certain tries; if they had been able to click in attack, the match would have been over by half-time.

Perhaps that's what Provan let them know in the sheds, because it was a different Sharks team that ran onto the Sydney Cricket Ground in the second half. Four minutes in and the Sharks were on the board via penalty goal for Manly being offside. Four minutes after that, Cronulla took the lead as second rower Eric Archer avoided the nudie run by scoring his first try of the season. And it was a cracker too; Paul Khan made a break, passed the ball to Pierce then Mullane and onto the winger with the surfie hair in Rick Bourke.

Bourke was pulled down just short of the line and then a lucky bat back of an errant pass by Mullane landed in Archer's hands. The Manly defence had already written off Archer as an attacking option because they kept pursuing across field expecting the second rower to pass the ball along the line.

Instead, Archer stepped off his left foot to get inside the overchasing Manly defence and then found that step had opened up a gap; all he had to do was sprint to the line. With the Rogers conversion making it 7-4, the Sharks had turned things around in the first eight minutes of the second half

Soon after Manly had a chance to level the scores, via a Mooney try in the corner. But desperate defence from Mullane on the diving Mooney knocked the ball loose. Cronulla made them pay for the botched try, with Chamberlin again slipping straight through the bewildered Manly line, before offloading for Mullane to score – 12-4 to the Sharks.

The Sea Eagles knew they were in trouble by this stage, and went for the tool of those otherwise out of

1978

luck – the trick play. In this case it was the wall; three attackers stand with their backs to the defence and the ball is passed to them. Then all three turn at once and run at the tacklers, hoping to confuse them as to who has the ball – of course, sometimes none of them do, because behind the wall the ball has been passed to a support player.

It didn't work the first time; the defence ragdolled support player Gibbs five metres behind the wall. Nor did it work the second time, with all three forwards in the wall smashed by the Sharks. They got a glimmer of hope via a Simon Booth try in the corner to set the scoreline at 12-7. That hope was snuffed out a few minutes later when Sharks half Steve Hansard broke through threadbare defence five metres on his side of halfway before flicking onto Kneen, who managed to run 15-20 metres without a hand being laid on him. As Manly closed in he passed to Rogers who set sail for the line and put it down under the posts – 17-7 to the Sharks. "The Manly defence is appalling," Rex Mossop said on the Channel 7 coverage. "There are other adjectives but that will do."

A late try to Ian Martin brought a veneer of respectability to the score, making it 17-12 – but the match was over by that stage. The Sharks, who nobody rated a chance, had knocked over the competition favourites.

After the match it was revealed Stares, Pierce and Kneen all took the field with cases of the flu. Mullane had been dosed up on pain killers for a groin injury he carried into the match, which club doctor Peter Malouf had said had been handicapping him in defence. "He can stretch out but when he props he feels it," the doc said. "If Cronulla can win on Saturday and go straight into the grand final two weeks later you'll see a much fitter and more confident Mullane in defence."

What Manly wanted to see was Hartley in the middle for the minor semi, making no secret of their dislike of Danzey's handling of the Sharks-Manly match. They claimed Danzey was over the play the ball when Manly was in possession but back with the Sea Eagles in defence; which resulted in them being pinged offside five times to the Sharks zero.

The criticism was unfounded; the match footage showed Danzey standing over the ruck for both sides. They were on much more solid ground with the complaint that Gibbs was tackled without the ball while chasing through a kick – that was as plain as day and it's hard to fathom how Danzey and his touch judges all missed it.

1978

That call for Hartley to referee the following week set the wheels in motion for an infamous moment in finals history.

Minor Preliminary Semi-Final

Canterbury vs Parramatta

Sydney Cricket Ground

Sunday, August 27

This semi saw a clash between two sides on the rise. They would go on to dominate the 1980s, both winning four premierships. The Eels threepeated in 1981-83 and picked up another in 1986 while the Dogs took it all in 1980, 1984-85 and 1988.

In the 1978 season the Dogs hadn't done a victory lap of the Sydney Cricket Ground for more than 30 years, while the Eels hadn't won a single title since they joined the NSW comp in 1947. So both fans were hoping this could be the year, though one of them was guaranteed to go home disappointed as the battle

1978

between fourth and fifth on the ladder was sudden death.

The smart money was on the Bulldogs as the team that would be heading off on Mad Monday the next day. Canterbury had not beaten the Eels in the home and away rounds and the bookies figured the Eels would be too strong. Dogs coach Ted Glossop seemed to agree; back in May he'd tagged Parramatta as the team to beat in 1978. "My opinion hasn't changed, but it's now a week-to-week survival game for both of us," he said in the week leading up to Sunday's clash.

He also had to deal with rumours of disquiet within the Canterbury camp following its poor form in the weeks before the finals. They'd lost to Cronulla and Easts, struggled against St George and had that shameful last-round draw against the poor Panthers. No matter which way you looked at it, that wasn't an ideal lead-up to the finals.

Glossop went on to scotch any rumours of dissension or that team selection was out of his hands. "Yes, I've read the stories and I've heard the talk but it is a load of rubbish," he said. "I've never been restricted in who I pick. No-one is twisting my arm. This is a happy club."

He did have problems with a few players. One of

them was long-serving prop Bill Noonan, who had been out injured since Round 19. Glossop named Noonan in the side to take on Parra, desperately hoping he'd be right by the weekend. "I haven't coached a better one and having him back is a real boost for us," the coach said.

The club also had concerns for forward Steve Hage, not because of injury but over fears the Eels might try and get under the hot-headed second-rower's skin. "I have no doubt Hage will receive special attention from the Parramatta forwards," Glossop said. "Hage gets more attention from opposition players than other forwards. But he is a tough, intelligent footballer and he won't retaliate."

Canterbury club secretary Peter Moore joined the chorus, claiming Hage's reputation as a tough guy meant that opponents felt they could put in a few cheap shots and not be pinged by the referee. Moore pointed to a recent match where he said Hage had been punched in several tackles but the only caution handed out by the ref was to Hage himself.

The secretary had gone so far as to talk to the referee's boss about getting fair treatment for Hage. Despite the latter controversy that would surround Hartley, the Dogs figured he'd do a good job of handling

1978

the cheap shots on Hage. "We're happy with Greg Hartley's appointment as referee," Moore said, "and I'm sure he'll handle any situation very fairly."

They would have a different view of Hartley after the full-time siren.

Parramatta had a better lead-in to Sunday's semi with centre Cronin winning his second straight Rothmans medal. With Ray Higgs winning in 1976 it gave the Eels a threepeat. In 1977 Cronin won with 25 points but in '78 gapped the field on 32 points, with second-placed Rod Reddy a long way back on 21 points. Manly's Johnny Gibbs would have finished second with 27 points, but a send-off for tripping against Souths in Round 8 ruled him ineligible, despite not being suspended by the judiciary.

The win was a fair reward for Cronin's massive pointscoring tally, which sat at 260 points heading into the finals. It seemed inevitable that he would break Souths' Eric Simms' record of 265 in a single season set in 1969 (but Simms' tally included 19 field goals in a time when they were worth two points).

Cronin did put a scare through Eels officials in the hours before the Rothmans ceremony. That's when they found out, only the day before the last-round clash with

Newtown, Cronin was playing footy on a muddy ground at Berry. It was a charity match the centre had put together to help a family whose father was ill and mother had been in a serious car accident.

"Cronin decided to put on a seven-a-side game in the hope of raising money for the family," the *Daily Mirror* reported. "He played the game in pouring rain, scored the winning try, kicked goals and raised $2000."

The news freaked out the Eels officials, who may have been put in a difficult position had Cronin been injured in a park footy match on the eve of the finals.

The Eels had hit a patch of form in the last few weeks before the finals, beating Penrith, Souths and Newtown by a combined 143 points to 35. But, were they to make it all the way and win their first grand final, they would have to rewrite history. No team had ever won the comp from where they sat – fifth spot. "I know the premiership hasn't been won by a side playing from fourth or fifth spot," said Ray Price in another of those ghostwritten newspaper columns, "but we'll change all that."

He didn't agree with the bookies' overwhelming favouritism, giving Canterbury an 11.5-point start, because he wasn't sure the Eels had that many points in them. "Canterbury play the type of game that can make

1978

it hard for you to score," he said. "I don't expect an avalanche of tries similar to the past two games but I don't expect to be beaten either."

In Dogs captain George Peponis' own ghostwritten piece, he admitted they had problems with consistency. "Our main trouble is that we struggle against the lowly teams. When the pressure has been on, we've usually played well. I know Parramatta have beaten us twice this year but that doesn't mean we can't beat them on Sunday."

At the coin toss before the start of the match, Price made the surprising call to run into a strong wind. The general wisdom is that you take the wind when it's there for it may die down by the time the teams switched ends. So he was probably a little relieved when the sides went in 7-7 at the break. But the second half was only eight minutes old when Parramatta made a costly blunder. Pressing on the Canterbury line Price opted not to kick for goal after Hartley awarded a penalty. A few tackles later, Steve Mortimer put the Dogs ahead with an intercept, running 90 metres to score. Mortimer, who was back in the No7 jersey after an odd decision by Glossop saw him at five-eighth for the previous nine games, had also laid on the kick for Steve Gearin's first-half try.

And the man they called Turvey wasn't quite done; five minutes later he slipped out of a half-dozen tackles to score next to the posts. It gave the Dogs a 15-7 lead with just over 23 minutes to play. The scribes had started to pencil in Mortimer for their man of the match. It was no small feat that he was even on the field; he had been struggling with asthma and chest pains – after that 90-metre intercept, he went to the sidelines to get a shot of Ventolin. "It's the first time I've had chest pains and I'm going to have X-rays tomorrow," he said after the game. "I don't know they affected me that much but they were a bit of a worry."

Then a complete nobody turned the game, scoring two tries in eight minutes. Forward Greg Heddles joined Parramatta from the Newcastle club Waratah-Mayfield that season but didn't play his first game in the competition proper until the last round (he got some minutes in a pre-season match and one Amco Cup fixture). "I came back from suspension to play a full game against Newtown last week," Heddles explained. "I was a bit upset after that game as we beat them 62-18 and I was one of only four players who didn't score a point."

He made up for that in the semi, coming on the field in the 48th minute to replace John Baker, who left the

1978

field to get a cut over his eye stitched up. Eleven minutes later he went wide of the ruck and crashed over, then in the 67th minute he was on the end of a Grahame Olling off-load for his second try. In just eight minutes, Heddles – who would play only one more match for Parramatta – snuffed out the Dogs chances, setting up a 17-15 lead. In the 72nd minute Cronin killed them off with a try in the corner, for a personal tally of 13 points – more than enough to take him past Simms' 1969 mark.

"It's nice to have broken such outstanding records but I don't think about those sorts of things in a game," Cronin said. "I just play along with the team and pick up the points whenever I can."

Glossop's fears about the Parramatta Eels had come to pass. After the match he tipped them as the frontrunners for the title. "They are a beautifully balanced side and they stick together, which is the unfailing sign of a class team," he said. "Even when they fell behind in the second half, they never argued among themselves, as some teams do. I was sitting on the sideline and you could hear them urging and encouraging each other."

Canterbury, who had praised Hartley before the match, changed their tune. There was some grumbling about the penalty count, which heavily favoured

Parramatta 11-4 (including 7-1 in the second half). "That was where we lost the match," secretary Peter Moore said. On top of that, the club alleged an unnamed Eels forward had kneed and kicked lock Graeme Hughes out of the match. He had gone down twice during the first half and couldn't come out for the second stanza, being replaced by Geoff Robinson. Hughes complained twice to Hartley, pointing out the Eels player. Hughes' teammates claimed the referee's response was to dismiss the issue, saying "there is not a malicious bone in that bloke's body".

Hartley also came in for criticism over his apparent awarding of a try to Geoff Gerard. Spectators, commentators and even the touch judges thought he had awarded the try, pointing to the spot, despite a blatant knock-on. He quickly corrected his signal to call the knock-on. *Rugby League Week* columnist Son of Max labelled Hartley "the best of a bad bunch of referees" and called on refs' boss Eric Cox to put him in his place (the columnist also suggested Hartley had twice miscounted tackles, though didn't say which team benefited).

The columnist wouldn't have been happy with Cox's actions, which was a weak defence of his referee. "I have no doubt Hartley lost control of his arm as he blew the

1978

whistle," Cox said

Major Semi-Final
Wests vs Cronulla
Sydney Cricket Ground
Saturday, September 2

The competition's battlers in recent years, Western Suburbs had an eye on making it all the way through to the grand final as a way of clearing their debts. The club had brought up coach Roy Masters from the under 23s, where he guided the team to the premiership in 1977, in part because he'd agreed to delay payment until they could afford to pay him. Going into 1978, the leagues club had cut its grant by $35,000 from last season's $130,000. The mid-year sponsorship from Victa brought in a much-needed $35,000 but the club was still in a hole.

In part it was the unexpected success of the 1978 side

that landed the club in what the *Daily Mirror* said was at least $70,000 in debt. Wests treasurer Bill Beaver revealed the club had budgeted to spend $380,000 over the 1978 season. "The $380,000 expenditure was budgeted on winning 13 games," Beaver said. "But we won 16 and drew another which is counted as a win in paying our players match bonuses." Winning too many matches blew out the budget.

"We won only seven games last year, so our match fee bonuses have more than doubled. We now need to make the grand final to clear ourselves of all debt."

Part of the plan to get to the grand final included an intensive training camp at the Nirimba navy base at Quakers Hill before heading to the SCG to watch the Cronulla-Manly final. Another part was trying to stop big prop John Donnelly from eating and drinking too much. To achieve that Masters sent him off to see the family in Gunnedah.

"Donnelly is in Gunnedah for his own good and the good of the side," Masters said. "He's fit and I want him to stay that way. Donnelly is a single man and I wanted him on a special diet this week. The rest of the side are on the diet and I feel a lot more secure knowing John is at home with his parents eating the right type of food."

The Magpies' pre-match preparation also included

going to the movies. On the Monday before the major semi, Masters took the team out to see the Burt Reynolds' film *The Mean Machine* (also known as *The Longest Yard*), where a group of prisoners take on a team of wardens in a football match. Or, as Raudonikis put it, giving away the ending in the process, "it is about a team of baddies in jail who beat a crackerjack wardens team in a game of gridiron".

"We have been cast as the bad boys all year and even though we won the minor premiership, few of the critics give us a real chance of being premiers," the half added. "They'll change their minds on Saturday."

Sharks hooker John McMartin had a different view of Masters' choice of movie. "It's about stiff arms and people getting their necks broken … a film about brutality. That's not a bad preparation for a match, is it?"

The hooker was preparing for some brutality, still carrying the scars from the last-round match against Wests that decided the minor premiership. He figured he was going to get whacked in the first scrum on Saturday.

"The two second rowers did it in our match at Endeavour Field two weeks ago," McMartin said. "They punched and kicked, yet we had a player sent off. Roy Masters claims we started it. That's just a big con. I know

1978

who started it and I had bruises to show for it."

Masters responded by referring to the Kneen elbow that levelled Foster in that Endeavour match. "They started the trouble at Endeavour Field two weeks ago and paid the penalty," he said. "I hope they go for a repeat." It was part of the Masters mentality in 1978 – distract the opposition with the rough stuff, get them focused on looking for a square-up and then beat them with skill.

"We play rugby league as it was meant to be played – hard and tough. I'm not saying we don't throw the odd punch, but punching is rule of thumb. I have a pack of forwards who like to exert their authority by giving what they receive."

The Masters mind games seemed to be working too. Even Sharks coach Norm Provan took the bait. "Wests coach Roy Masters should put his own house in order first instead of branding my players thugs. Masters is psyching his players up to where they're now running out for games like mad dogs. Wests can either play football or have a brawl on Saturday. We will accommodate them whichever way they want to play it."

Comments like that were playing right into Masters' hands, giving him the material he needed to psyche up his team.

Wests captain John Dorahy said a focus for the black-and-white defence would be the edge where Rogers and Chamberlin so often cut through the Manly side a week earlier. Dorahy reckoned a centre he called 'the Rock' – aka Ron Giteau – was the answer.

"He is one of Sydney's most under-rated players," Dorahy said in a *Sun* column. "Few centres had outplayed Giteau this season and he's just the player to blot out brilliant attackers like Rogers and Chamberlin."

Sharks captain Rogers agreed with the assessment that one of his team's strengths was the speed of the outside backs. Implying Wests had a habit of standing offside, he said Cronulla would have to take advantage of any break that came their way because there wouldn't be as many as in the Manly match.

On the day of the match, the Wests players and their partners met at the leagues club and travelled to the Sydney Cricket Ground together. With about an hour to go before kick-off, Masters shut the dressing room door and began geeing up the troops. This hour would be crucial, Masters had said in the days before the match. "I'll know 15 minutes before kick-off if we are going to win or not," he said.

What Masters observed of his players in that period mustn't have been good. Despite running against the

1978

wind, the Sharks looked the far better team right from the start. Rick Bourke grounded a Rogers bomb over the line in the sixth minute but was called offside. Then Kneen blew a certain try after making a break and then ignoring Rogers in support with the line open.

In the 18th minute, they got it all together. A Rogers bomb was spilt by Rowles and Greg Pierce managed to ground the ball. With two minutes on the clock, Dorahy lobbed a low percentage pass to winger Buddy Cain. But it never got to Cain; Sharks winger Steve Edmonds snaffled the intercept and ran 50 metres to score. Dorahy could be seen in the background slamming his fist into the SCG turf in frustration.

The two scores sent the Sharks into the break 10-4 up; all Wests could manage were two penalty goals from Rowles.

Masters must have said something in the sheds at half-time, because Wests held out the Sharks and eventually levelled the score at 10-all in the 68th minute. The Magpies hadn't crossed the stripe though; all their points came from Rowles' boot. Wayne Smith thought he had scored in the 59th minute after chasing through a Dorahy kick, but ref Danzey said he'd failed to force the ball.

Wests had help in levelling up via a very one-sided

penalty count from Danzey in the second half; at one stage it was 8-1 to them and ultimately finished at 12-4 for the half. Three penalties in just six minutes allowed Wests to tie it up.

With a grandstand finish looking likely, Danzey evened up the ledger late by awarding the Sharks a pair of penalties that Rogers slotted between the posts to get home 14-0 and book themselves a grand final berth.

There was some rough stuff and controversy in the match. Sorenson's replacement Stares was pinged for whacking Dorahy and, as the penalty was awarded, he raced over to Danzey and started rolling up the sleeve of his jersey. He'd insisted he'd just been bitten and wanted to show the ref the bite mark.

The *Rugby League Week* match report described them as "savage wounds", and there were reports of Pierce and Bourke also claiming to have been bitten. In a curious decision, refs boss Cox dismissed it all very quickly. "I don't think there is a biter. I've played the game … players grip you by the fingers and stick them into you. That's what happened. It's time the players shut up."

With Dorahy being hit by Stares, the speculation was rife that he had bitten the young prop. "I saw Stares race towards referee Jack Danzey and lift up a sleeve on his jumper," Dorahy said. "He showed him a mark on his arm. I don't know how he got it but I do know I did not bite him."

The biggest moment in the match after Pierce hung out an arm and felled Donnelly. Danzey had a look at it and merely issued a running caution to the Sharks captain. But two tackles later both touch judges ran on to report the incident, and Pierce was sent off. The decision riled up a section of Sharks supporters, who had already thrown oranges and dry ice Danzey's way following an earlier decision.

In the sheds after the match, a disconsolate Pierce didn't want to talk to the press, though Provan figured it would all be sweet. "The referee saw what happened and took no action other than to caution Greg on the run," he said.

For Cronulla's sake it really did have to be all sweet. With Sorenson already gone for the finals series, the Sharks could ill afford to lose their captain, who had 10 seasons under his belt and had captained his country in a match against New Zealand earlier in the season. He was one of the most experienced Sharks in a team full of younger players and his guidance would be vital if the Sharks were to win the competition in 1978.

The judiciary didn't help the Sharks, handing Pierce a

four-match suspension on the Monday night after the match. The club immediately planned an appeal, which required new evidence to be found. This included a photo by *Rugby League Week* photographer John Elliott, taken at the moment of impact. The paper splashed it on the front page of its next edition. To modern eyes, it didn't seem to exonerate Pierce; it showed him with his left arm crooked around John Donnelly's neck from behind. It looks for all the world like a high tackle, but the suspension was for a *head*-high tackle, so the Sharks must have felt the photo showed no head contact.

The club also felt the fact that Danzey and both touch judges were dropped to reserve grade was a sign the referee's boss wasn't happy with their performance.

The appeals committee didn't think much of the new evidence and confirmed the four-week ban at a Friday night meeting. That led Pierce to briefly considering following the lead of Les Boyd, and taking the matter to the NSW Equity Court. Though there was no coverage of such a case, which suggests Pierce didn't go through with it.

1978

Minor Semi Final

Manly vs Parramatta

Sydney Cricket Ground

Sunday, September 3

The Manly-Parramatta rivalry was immortalised in a pair of Toohey's ads, both of which featured Ray Price scoring the first try. Based on the players in the Eels side, the jersey sponsors (Parramatta – none, Manly – Pioneer) and the fact we see Allan Thompson and Price score, it seems most likely the first of the ads was based on the 1977 Round 4 clash, won by Parra 24-15.

That rivalry was built in the 1970s, with this finals clash expected by some to be a rough affair, perhaps with a bit of skirting of the rules. According to Parramatta coach Terry Fearnley – who was also unimpressed Hartley's penalty count went 12-5 the way of Manly, 8-1 in the second half – that's exactly what happened. In the first of the finals matches to end in a draw, Fearnley claimed Manly players hit half Graham Murray, prop Bob Jay and last-match star Heddles with high tackles. The half left the field with a probable broken jaw, Jay a likely broken cheekbone and Heddles was suffering concussion.

"Each was hit in a blatant illegal tackle," the coach said. "Only Jay has any chance of playing on Wednesday, and that's only a slight one.

"Apparently you've got to be one of the favoured clubs in this business, and we're not. After all the talk recently I thought the game was going to be cleaned up. But it seems to be open slather – if it is we should be told."

Jay agreed with Fearnley, saying his cheekbone injury came from a late elbow. "I can't understand how the linesman missed it," he said. "The same player got Greg Heddles, who replaced me."

Jay didn't name that player, but the next day, Manly's John Harvey outed himself. One of his tackles had left Jay lying on the SCG turf and the other rattled Heddles. In the replay of the tackle, it did appear there was a raised elbow from Harvey, and Heddles seemed knocked out

1978

before he hit the ground.

"I haven't been named by anyone but it is obvious they are talking about me," Harvey told *The Sun*.

"I wasn't cautioned and no linesman came onto the field to report me. League's a tough game and that's the way I like to tackle in such an important match. But I tackled within the rules on Sunday. It would be senseless to risk high tackles after all the recent publicity."

Going into the match, the Sea Eagles named Eadie as their number one goal kicker, following John Gray's poor effort against Cronulla. "Eadie has kicked us to some vital wins in big matches before and is a proven pressure kicker in grand finals," Frank Stanton said, adding he had ordered the fullback to go through two hours of kicking practice a day in the week leading up to the Parramatta match.

It wasn't a success – Eadie missed all five of his shots at goal, forcing Stanton to give the kicking duties back to Gray. With both sides scoring three tries, the match really came down to goalkicking, and if Eadie landed just one of those, there would have been no need for that now infamous mid-week replay.

Early on it looked as though it would be the Eels ensuring there would be no replay. In the first half they looked the far better side and walked off after the first

40 up 8-3. That lead was extended to 13-3 eight minutes into the second stanza, when Geoff Gerard scored and Cronin converted. All Parramatta had to do was keep defending and Manly were done.

But Allan Thompson managed to find some space for winger Simon Booth with a long pass. The winger ran 35 metres down the sideline to score, which started the Manly comeback. A Gray penalty goal put the score at 13-8.

With 11 minutes to go, Booth bamboozled Neville Glover and off-loaded to the hotfooted Russel Gartner to score. Gray kicked the two and the scoreline that had looked so good for the Eels was now locked up at 13-13. Both sides had their chances to break the deadlock; Cronin's field-goal attempt was charged down, as was Manly's effort from Steve Martin (charged down by John Peard, who had earlier pulled off a trysaving cover tackle on Gartner).

With the league having ruled out extra time after copping criticism for last year's St George-Parramatta grand final, when the full-time hooter sounded, it meant both sides would be back a few days later to do it all again.

That led some pundits – and players – to decide the need for a replay had handed the 1979 premiership to either Cronulla or Wests. *The Mirror*'s Bill Mordey wrote of the Wests players leaving the SCG laughing after the draw, sure Manly and Parramatta would batter each other out of premiership contention.

"Parramatta and Manly have almost certainly kissed goodbye to hopes of winning the 1978 premiership," *The Mirror*'s Mordey wrote in his match report.

Former Sea Eagle Bob Fulton also figured it was curtains for his old club. "Parramatta and Manly are the best teams in the premiership and neither can do a lap of honour on grand final day," Bozo wrote in *The Sun*. "The league's decision to cease the former method of playing an extra 10 minutes each way in case of a draw at full-time has killed the chances of both teams.

"It's a mammoth task to ask a side to play a semi-final replay on Wednesday and then back up in a final three days later.

"Wests must be laughing – they have virtually been presented with a clear passage into the big one."

Minor Semi Final Replay

Manly vs Parramatta

Sydney Cricket Ground

Wednesday, September 6

This wouldn't be the first time in a finals series two teams were forced back to the SCG because of a draw. The same thing happened – in the same match even – in 1973 when Newtown and St George met in the minor semi. The score was 10-10 at full-time and so 20 minutes of extra time was played.

One penalty goal each was all the teams could muster up in extra time. In a heartbreaker for the Dragons, the Jets' penalty goal came right as time was running out and locked things up at 12-12. So they met again at the Sydney Sports Ground (where the Allianz Stadium car

1978

park now is) on Tuesday for the rematch, won by the Jets 8-5.

This Manly-Parramatta replay wasn't even the only one in 1978 – or the only one that involved the Eels. Ahead of last Sunday's Cronulla-Wests match, the Eels reserve grade side took on Balmain, where the Tigers led 3-0 for most of the match before Parramatta scored an equaliser four minutes from full-time.

They had to return to the SCG on the same day as the Manly-Parra replay – likely making Parramatta the only side ever to have two teams playing a finals replay match on the same day. And the reserve-grade replay almost ended in a draw as well, until Tigers winger Wayne Miranda landed a massive 50-metre penalty goal. That would see the Eels reserves face off against St George in the preliminary final the following week.

Which also ended in a draw. The Eels looked like scraping into the grand final 11-10, until Dragons' half Lee Pomfret landed a match-tying field goal seconds before full-time. So back the Eels reserves went to the SCG for its second replay. But this time the toll of four matches in 10 days was too much – St George rolled them 22-9.

People didn't know it at the time, but a future star

was making his run-on debut in the first-grade replay, though not in his preferred position. Fearnley was dealing with casualty ward full of players in the wake of the Manly match on the weekend.

That injury list saw Fearnley pull aside a kid named Peter Sterling at training early that week and told him he'd be playing fullback. It showed how skint the Eels were; Mark Levy was out injured – having managed to hurt his back in the Under 23s semifinal after kicking the ground behind the ball during a conversion attempt. Fearnley's other option was Ken Hey, who had injured himself in the dying seconds of the top grade semifinal a few days ago. So an 18-year-old with a single game under his belt – a bench spot in the Round 18 match against St George – got the nod for the semi replay.

Outwardly he showed confidence, perhaps too much confidence. He told the papers the Eels would win by 20. "I'm really looking forward to being in the game," he said on the Monday before the re-match. Sterling said he was ready for Manly to put up plenty of bombs, then a new attacking ploy in the league. "They can kick as much as they like. It's easier to play with the ball than without it."

After the match, Fearnley praised the efforts of the teenager. "He'll go places," the coach accurately predicted. "He's one of the best I have seen." Though Sterling himself would later not be too impressed with his own efforts.

"When I look back on that challenging day I know now that I wasn't ready for it," Sterling said in his autobiography. "I played to my ability but unfortunately my ability at that time didn't justify me being where I was."

Levy and Hey weren't the only ones out of action for Parramatta in the replay. Murray was gone, so was Heddles and they'd lost hooker Ron Hilditch. That last withdrawal meant lower grade player Kevin Webb – with all of five first grade matches under his belt, none of them in 1978 – had to face the Australian hooker Max Krilich in the scrums. They also had the extra headache of their reserve grade side playing its own replay on the Wednesday, limiting their replacement options.

Manly were dealing with a few casualties as well; they were without Johnny Gibbs and forward Ian Martin, with John Gray and Krilich carrying injuries into the match.

The mid-week replay led to calls from some quarters that the league should move the preliminary final to Sunday. "This is the only common sense move if Parramatta or Manly aren't to be served up as wounded, weakened prey for Wests," the *Mirror*'s Bill Mordey wrote. But the league said no, because they'd already sold more than 1000 reserved seats for the Saturday fixture and felt some of those spectators wouldn't be able to rock up on the Sunday.

The short turnaround for the replay meant there wasn't much preparation the teams could do. Stanton ordered the Manly players to take the Tuesday off work for an "office hours day", where they'd have a light training run and spend from 9am to 5pm together. "We'll stick together for the day talking about the game and tactics to be used," Stanton said.

Parramatta, on the other hand, were preparing for some biff, and promising to match it with Manly – despite their coach's objection to the rough stuff.

"Parramatta players said they were sick and tired of the treatment they had received in big games for the past three seasons without official action being taken against the offenders," the *Mirror*'s back page said. "They claimed they had not forgotten the 1976 grand final against Manly when skipper Ray Higgs received a broken jaw, last year's grand final replay and Sunday's semi, in which key players were put out of action."

1978

There must have been a lot of empty offices on the Wednesday of the replay, as people called in sick to go to the game. The crowd for the weekend semi was 30,850, but thousands more turned up for the mid-week replay. The official crowd number was 42,678, which would have been an unplanned boost to the league's coffers. Even the workers building a new stand at the SCG took a break to watch the game from the scaffolding.

The match started the same way as Sunday's minor semi, with Parramatta looking like dead certs to move forward to play Wests a few days later. Geoff Gerard raced through some flimsy defence to score the first try, which was followed by another first-half three-pointer to Glen West. With both sides landing a penalty goal, the Eels went into the sheds at half-time up 8-2.

But there was one difference in this match; the Parramatta players seemed keen to ignore Fearnley's edict to leave out the rough stuff and let the referee handle things. There was a lot of pushing and shoving, a few punches thrown and touch judges coming on to report players four times. Tempers really flared late in the first half, with West and Tom Mooney brawling in the corner after the Manly centre pulled off a try-saving tackle, and then continued in-goal with Price and Eadie coming in conflict. It saw the touchies come on and led to Hartley sending Price from the field. While he would later dodge any suspension, the TV replays clearly showed the Eels captain having a swing at Eadie's head while the Manly fullback was lying on the ground. Obviously the 1970s were a different era, where clear footage of a haymaker that connected didn't warrant a suspension.

In the second half, despite playing a man down, the Eels stretched out the lead to 11-2 with a try to Neville Glover. It was at that point, Stanton later admitted, the coach thought his team was gone. His mood couldn't have been helped when the Sea Eagles lost their one-man advantage with John Gray being sent off. Hartley really had no other option; the prop had whacked Bob Jay in the face with a blatant elbow. There was no attempt at a tackle; Jay ran at Gray with the ball and Gray cocked the elbow and hit him in the face.

But it was from that moment that the Eels wilted. John Harvey scored a converted try to bring the score to 11-7 and later Gartner scored a 75-metre try that should not have been allowed by the Eels defence. From a scrum on the Manly quarter, Gartner turned on the speed down the blind side and was barely impeded by the Parramatta defence. Eadie's kick hit the upright but

1978

the score was now 11-10; the Sea Eagles who looked done and dusted were storming home – just like in Sunday's minor semi.

Then came the try that took Manly ahead and would be the source of controversy after the game, and for decades later. Replacement Ray Branighan put up a rushed kick on what everyone thought was the last tackle, the ball was flipped back towards Manly during the contest and Steve Martin happened to be right there to catch it and plant the ball without a defender laying a hand on him. Eadie converted to give the Sea Eagles a 15-11 lead.

That was extended to 17-11 in the dying stages when Peard gave away a penalty close to the posts. Peard yanked his arm out of the tackle and swung at the Manly player, then pointed down to his arm as if to suggest he'd been bitten. And that's exactly what he claimed had happened, saying he had been conned into giving away the penalty.

"The player bit me," Peard said after the match, "but I should have known better. I should have copped the bite. But it's a terrible sensation having someone's mouth wrapped around your hand. You can't help yourself – it's a natural reaction to lash out."

It took less than 24 hours for one of the biggest controversies in rugby league to break, thanks to a Blacktown woman. Parramatta fan Dorothy Williams thought something was wrong in the lead-up to Martin's try and so went back to count the tackles – and there were seven of them.

"I couldn't believe it," she said. "I've often seen wrong tackle counts but this one was so vital." So she rang the sports desk at *The Sun*, who were only too happy to accept such a cracking yarn.

"Really, I did it for the footballers," Williams said. "I wanted everyone to know that our Parramatta footballers who tried so hard were defeated like that."

The Sun splashed Hartley's "incredible blunder" on the back page, with photos from the TV coverage of every tackle. They gave Hartley a call, who claimed to have been surprised the winning try was scored on the seventh tackle. "As far as I was concerned it was a fair try scored inside the number of allowable tackles," he said, even though it obviously wasn't.

Worse was to come for Hartley. One of *The Sun*'s sports journos got the Channel 7 match footage and had the job of counting all the tackles. It was worth the effort because they found another story to kick along the

1978

controversy.

"Referee Greg Hartley erred in his tackle count six other times apart from the vital mistake which brought Manly's winning try against Parramatta in Wednesday's semifinal," the back page stated.

"Further TV evidence of Wednesday's semifinal replay has shown that Parramatta received only five tackles on three occasions."

Hartley had also awarded seven-tackle sets to Manly three times, including when the match-winner was scored, and five tackles once. All up Hartley had not been able to count to six at least seven times.

The news sparked death threats to Hartley, who said he had to unplug his home phone so he could get to sleep. "I am not taking the threats seriously because they are probably being made by some disgruntled league fan."

They weren't the only one disgruntled; Parramatta was understandably aggrieved and lodged a protest on the Friday to have the result annulled and a replay of the replay be scheduled. If upheld, it would have created headaches for the league; the semifinal would have to be played on the Saturday and the final moved to Sunday (the Eels had also considered taking out an injunction to stop the final from going ahead). Also, it left the fate of

Ray Price unclear; he had been sent off but not had his day in front of the judiciary, so would he be eligible to play in the replay of the replay?

Wests, no fan of Hartley, also weighed in with a call for Danzey to be appointed as man in the middle for the final. "We believe that Hartley is far too excitable to handle the final," said Wests secretary Gary Russell. "We realise Hartley has already been appointed for the final but we want a change made.

"We fully intend to have a conference with Hartley before the kick-off on Saturday. And we will certainly make sure our skipper Tommy Raudonikis is fully aware of his constitutional rights on the field. As skipper he has the right to protest against any decisions he considers to be wrong or incompetent."

Manly boss Ken Arthurson kicked the Eels when they were down, labelling them a pack of whingers. "They whinged after last year's grand final, they whinged after our first semi and they are still at it," he said. "Personally, I'm disappointed at their carry on. In this game you have to learn to accept your defeats with your victories."

Something that was easy to say when the seven-tackle set helped your team to victory.

Unsurprisingly, the league rejected Parramatta's

1978

appeal to have the result annulled, taking just 12 minutes to reach a decision on the night before the scheduled Wests-Manly final. What was surprising, and still surprising today, is that no further action was taken. Despite a litany of errors by Hartley, the league kept his ranking as the top referee and allowed him to continue to control matches in the finals series - thereby leaving the door open for more controversy.

Some journalists criticised the Eels' attempt to have the match annulled. The *Sun-Herald*'s Alan Clarkson. "Despite the statements that they owed the appeal to their supporters, one could be forgiven for believing that Parramatta could not take the defeat," Clarkson wrote.

In the same column he said he felt sorry for the "flamboyant" Hartley. "He refereed last Sunday's Parramatta and Manly game and the replay on Wednesday and I doubt if there have been two more exciting matches this season. It seemed inevitable Hartley would referee the grand final, but on Thursday the world fell in on him."

There has been a lingering suspicion that the fix was in; that the repeated incorrect tackle counts – and the appointment of Hartley to Manly's finals matches was proof of some conspiracy to deliver the premiership to the Sea Eagles. And conspiracies are always more juicy than boring reality.

Hartley was more likely elevated back to the top grade due to the Wests-Manly punch-up at Lidcombe earlier in the season and the black eye it gave the code. Hartley was the sort of ref who would stand up to the players and it was entirely possible the league saw in him someone who could reduce the rough stuff on the field.

Also, the idea of any conspiracy in the minor semi replay would have to extend beyond Hartley himself to include the touch judges. After all, they came onto the field several times in the first half to report players, prompting action from Hartley. And sometimes, Hartley chose to only issue a warning rather than giving a penalty. That the touchies were also part of the fix is just too far-fetched.

When it comes to those tackle counts, it's far more likely that Hartley just screwed up. As Ray Chesterton said in a history of the Sea Eagles, he was "always a flawed referee whose technical mastery of the job was questionable at times". This was a referee who, in a 1977 Easts-St George match, awarded a field goal to Bob Fulton even though he had punted the ball and it went between the posts. Hartley simply had not seen the kick itself and awarded a field goal.

And that go-ahead try scored on the seventh tackle?

1978

Well, there's no guarantee the same thing wouldn't have happened on the sixth tackle anyway. Manly were always going to put up a bomb on the last, and with that tactic being a new one in the late 1970s, defenders still hadn't worked out an effective way to neutralise it. So the Sea Eagles could well still have scored that try to take the lead.

Finally, blaming the tackle counts for Manly's win allowed one crucial factor to go under the radar – Cronin's goal kicking. The Rothmans Medal winner had a shocker of a performance in the replay, kicking just one from five. More accurate kicking could have seen the Sea Eagles give up any attempt to chase down the scoreline.

Add to that his effort in the weekend's minor semi and, across to the two matches, he kicked just three out of 10 attempts. Then there was his missing of a clutch kick late in the 1977 grand final, with the score tied at 9-all. It was suggestive of a player who hadn't quite gotten the nerves under control when it came to important kicks. Though it seemed to be something he had well and truly dealt with by the time of the Eels' years of domination in the 1980s.

<u>Preliminary Final</u>

Wests vs Manly

Sydney Cricket Ground

Saturday, September 9

The Newtown Jets had a season to forget. Actually, they'd had quite a few seasons to forget since their last finals appearance in 1973 (the year they adopted the Jets name), where they were knocked out by Cronulla in the final. If that made fans of the inner-city club feel like good times were around the corner - they'd last won it all in 1943 - they were wrong. The team tumbled back down the ladder in 1974 and, a few seasons later in 1976 they started a run of three straight wooden spoons.

In '76, they had a 3-19 record, lost 20 games and won just two the year after and in 1978 won the same number,

1978

lost 19 and had a 6-all draw with St George. The Jets were in last place by Round 6 and stayed there for the rest of the season, during which time they were on the wrong end of some big scorelines. Parra beat them 35-6, the Sharks put the cleaners through them 44-0, the Dragons won 39-8 and then Parra handed out another thumping in the last round – by which time the Jets players were clearly thinking about the off-season – with the scoreboard reading 62-18 at full-time. If fans were desperate for any bright side, there was the Amco Cup match where they beat Past Patrician Bros 49-0.

As an aside, this was back in the day when an insane number of teams took part in the midweek comp. The 1978 comp had a frankly astonishing 38 teams; as well as the NSW teams, all the sides in the Brisbane comp took part, six more teams from regional Queensland as did Monaro, Newcastle, Riverina, two teams from New Zealand and rep sides from WA and the Northern Territory. It was just so stupid.

Anyway, back to the Jets and the 1978 season. That saw the side score an average of nine points a game and let in 26 points. So, yeah, definitely a season to forget. As the finals started, the Jets board were out in the market on a very Manly-like spending spree – helped by the cash from club sponsor John Singleton.

One might think that a team that had finished last for the previous three seasons would be pushing poo uphill to sign anyone, but there was an influx of players – including some from 1978 finalists; Steve Hage and Bill Noonan from the Dogs and Wests' top pointscorer Peter Rowles and the Magpies' Steve Blyth. They also brought in Ted Goodwin from the Dragons (who only ended up playing seven matches, two of them from the bench before moving onto Wests), Queensland rep player John Ribot and Brian Hetherington from Dapto.

Canterbury boss Peter Moore was one to complain about Newtown's poaching, claiming it was "adding to the game's inflationary spiral". "The Newtown club has been an embarrassment to rugby league for a long time now and they will be an even bigger one if they hide behind their agents' activities," Moore said. "We would not attempt to match the method of the payment by the Newtown club."

Perhaps their most audacious bid was to poach two-time Rothmans medallist Mick Cronin once the Eels were out of the finals. In part because a helicopter was part of the deal. With the centre's contract with the Eels expiring at the end of the 1978 season, the Jets swooped in with a $50,000 offer, with the sweetener of helicopter rides to matches and training so the Gerringong-based

1978

Cronin didn't have to drive to Sydney several times a week.

"That's a heavy schedule for anyone let alone a top footballer," Singleton told the *Daily Mirror*, "and we want to relieve him of what must be quite a burden. I intend offering him the use of a private helicopter if he agrees to join our club. The way I see it the chopper may be just the bait to lure him away from Parramatta."

History showed the chopper wasn't able to woo Cronin, who stayed with the Eels until he retired in 1986.

When it came to match preparation for the 1978 final, there really wasn't a whole lot of time for Manly to sort things out. They'd won on Wednesday and then had just two free days before having to back up against Wests in the final. Even then there was the Parramatta appeal against the result; it wouldn't be clear who Manly's next opponent was until the night before the match, when the league ruled out another replay.

Still, Manly did find the time to call in what one paper called "a commando" to give a motivational talk, while the league sat to discuss Parramatta's appeal. "They were given the psych treatment of troops going into battle by the high-ranking officer who dropped into the ground by helicopter," the *Sunday Mirror* reported.

Part of the talk included a discussion of how there were few triumphs more satisfying than the one everyone said could not be done. That gelled with Manly's situation; having to play match after match, players carrying injuries, had led to most pundits writing off their chances. Surely, the pundits felt, the pressure and the strain would tell.

There were some Manly players feeling that pressure. The night before the clash with Manly, Allan Thompson hardly slept a wink. "I went to bed at 11.30 but tossed and turned all through the night," he said. "I couldn't get the match out of my head – you name it, I thought about it."

The Magpies had a more stable preparation for the final, though there would have been a hiccup over having to wait until the middle of the week to final out the identity of their opponent. Also, there was the ongoing contract negotiations with gun forward Les Boyd, who had a clause in his contract that allowed him to return to his home town of Cootamundra any time he wanted. In the week leading to the final, Boyd was suggesting he was thinking of doing exactly that once he married his fiancée Judy Luck at the end of the season.

"We're both country people but it is becoming increasingly difficult to keep turning down offers," Boyd

1978

said. "I hate city life and Judy isn't too keen to live in Sydney."

Wests had been trying to get Boyd to extend his contract for the previous two months, with secretary Gary Russell suggesting there would be big money involved. "They can set themselves up for life if Les signs a new contract for three or four years," Russell said.

The stand-off wouldn't be resolved until after the final, with Boyd agreeing to stay with Wests for the 1979 season on the Monday. That would end up being his last season in the black-and-white; in 1980 he would cross the bridge and play four seasons with Manly.

The Manly side was showing the signs of a team who had played just a few days ago. Injuries had become a problem, with a final line-up not established until 90 minutes before kick-off. One of those late starters was lock Ian Martin, who had been given up until the last minute to be declared fit to play. Also in trouble was Krilich and Randall, who had carried injuries into the last games and did so again against Wests.

As pretty much everyone would have expected, Wests started the game looking to intimidate Manly; the first penalty went to Manly after Raudonikis chose to grab a fistful of Stephen Knight's hair to try and bring him to ground in a gang tackle. Other tackles saw swinging arms, forearm jolts and knees in the tackle; if Hartley was really favouring Manly he had plenty of reasons to blow the pea out of the whistle, but only penalised Wests once in the early stages.

The Sea Eagles took the lead early after John Dorahy fumbled a Steve Martin bomb close to the dead-ball line. Allan Thompson, on his way to a man of the match effort, pounced on the loose ball. "I couldn't believe my eyes when Dorahy spilled that bomb," Thompson said. "He had it covered all the way and dropped it at my feet." With the Eadie conversion, Manly took the lead 5-0. Wests would later level with a try from a kick of their own, bulky winger Ron Giteau touching down.

As the clock ticked away the minutes to halftime, Manly looked like they were starting the feel the effects of playing their third match in less than a week. After a strong start where they stood up to the rough stuff from Wests, the Sea Eagles were a side desperately looking for the half-time break. Fortunately for them, the hooter sounded without any further change to the 5-5 scoreline.

After the break, the Manly side came back refreshed, with Thompson scoring his second after finding a diagonal seam through the Wests defence and scoring near the corner.

That was one of the moments that let the air out of the Wests side. Two others came in the form of disallowed tries. First Hartley ruled Geoff Foster was held up over the line; the second-rower didn't protest so he must have felt it was a fair call.

The second disallowed try has gone down in Wests folklore as an example of Hartley's shonky nature, though it is really nothing of the sort. Graeme O'Grady put up a bomb, there was a sea of hands reaching for the ball, which fell to the ground. O'Grady happened to be on the spot, picking it up cleanly to plant it over the line. But Hartley ruled no try. Since then, most notably in the documentary *The Fibros and the Silvertails*, Wests players have claimed Hartley ruled O'Grady off-side, which is obviously impossible given that he kicked the ball. It was held up as an example of how Hartley had it in for Wests and was favouring Manly.

However, it's not true, and all it takes to refute that is to watch the match footage. Hartley had called a knock-on and then packed a scrum. If O'Grady had been ruled offside, it would have been a penalty to Manly. A knock-on at this point is possible; there were at least four players contesting the bomb. In the absence of high-quality replays, it seems likely a Wests player did tap the ball forward.

From that point all the Magpies could manage was a solitary penalty goal to Peter Rowles. The side who had been smiling at the news of the mid-week replay, sure Manly would turn up to the final like lambs to the slaughter ended up losing 12-7. Losing both their finals matches, the minor premiers had blown their chance of making their first grand final since 1963 and winning their first premiership since 1952.

Part of the reason for the poor finals showing can be put down to the problem with the siege mentality Masters had created that season. Lidcombe Oval was their fortress; any teams travelling out that way on the weekend knew they were in for a rough match. The results spoke for themselves; they won all 11 home games in 1978. But a look at the away results tells a less convincing tale. When the Magpies had to travel, they couldn't bring the fortress with them. So they ended the regular season with a 5-5 record. And for the Magpies the vast expanse of the Sydney Cricket Ground was an away venue. They weren't at Lidcombe, able to ride the wave of the cheering partisan crowd.

Over in the other team sheds was a team everyone had written off; not unjustifiably after playing mid-week.

1978

But the Manly side had somehow managed to play through injury to find themselves in the grand final. "It was a fantastic feeling out there," Thompson said. "It was a team effort based on sheer guts and will to win. I've never known spirit like it before. Everyone was playing his heart out for the bloke next to him."

Someone else who had a good game, according to the newspaper sports journos, was Hartley. His shocker just days earlier was seemingly forgotten, with journos choosing to praise the whistleblower's efforts. "Hartley shrugged off the worry of this three-day trial by TV in which he'd been pilloried for incorrect tackle counts in the replay," the *Sunday Mirror* reported. "Hartley had a top game and disallowed four tries – two to each side – because he was right on top of the play throughout."

Elsewhere in the Sunday papers, Peter Frilingos also praised Hartley's performance. "He made sure he let the game flow and cracked down on the odd offender, but above all he made sure the game was a classic final."

Grand Final

Cronulla vs Manly

Sydney Cricket Ground

Saturday, September 16

Amid all the drama of the mid-week replay and the seven tackles, pretty much everyone's attention had shifted away from the Sharks, who hadn't played since their major semi win over Wests two weeks ago. Though on the same weekend Wests played Manly, the Sharks officials did something really stupid – they organised a street parade through three of the suburbs of the shire.

"It was a remarkable turnout of the public to cheer the boys and wish them luck," said club secretary Arthur Winn. "It is difficult to estimate how many people watched the parade but there were thousands lined up at every stop they made."

Maybe it was an attempt to bring some attention to the Cronulla side, but they had clearly not learned from Parramatta, who did the same thing shortly before losing the 1976 grand final. Everyone knows you have a parade *after* you win the big one, not before. Going off early just gives the Footy Gods a chance to smite you.

Some fans were likely expecting a repeat of the last time these two sides met in a grand final. It was just five years ago so the 1973 decider was fresh in the memory of many.

"Every illegality was used in those 40 minutes of the first half and several times play exploded into a brawling mass of players," the *Sydney Morning Herald* reported on the 1973 grand final. "In one explosion about 20 players were involved at various parts of the field with a dozen milling around one spot. Every tackle in those hectic minutes was loaded with menace and was meant to damage. There were punches, kneeing and kicking as the rough play raged from one end of the field to the other."

Nineteen-year-old Sharks winger Steve Rogers called it "a brawl with a game breaking out in the middle." Players looked to settle scores from earlier matches, and

Sharks halfback Tommy Bishop went around provoking fights, relying on hard man Cliff Watson to clean them up.

Sharks lock Greg Pierce put the violence down to a mistake on the league's part. Rather than have the teams run out onto the field from the sheds, they warmed on the field for 15 minutes before running to the halfway line as they were introduced one by one. It was all taking too long, reckoned Pierce. "Tensions built up so much that when the game started they were released in a flurry.

In the lead-up to the 1978 decider, the newspapers were keen to cash in on the footy fans' love of the rough stuff. *The Sun* took advantage of having Peter Peters, who played for Manly in the 1973 bash-athon on staff to write two separate feature pieces on that match.

"Every time referee Keith Page and his linesmen broke up a fight in the 1973 grand final another brawl erupted a few yards away," Peters wrote. "You could hear bones crack after the thud of a boot went in. I thought 'what am I doing here?'."

Sharks coach Norm Provan was trying to play mind games with his rival Stanton by chopping and changing his line-up for the '78 grand final. First he decided to split up the dynamic centre pairing of Rogers and Chamberlin by training the former at lock for one session. Then he had Rogers at five-eighth, Barry Andrews at lock and youngster Chris Gardner with Chamberlin in the centres. Then Rogers was back in the No3, with Chamberlin moved to No6.

By Thursday, Provan had moved all his pieces back to their normal positions and brought in John Glossop to play lock. The coach's stated motivation behind all this was to try and replace suspended forward Greg Pierce. And then when he moved Rogers back to the centres it was because he felt opposite number Russel Gartner would be carrying an injury into the match.

But it was all rubbish; he was never going to split up the attacking partnership of Rogers and Chamberlin. And it really fooled no-one, though the sports journos ate it up as it gave them something else to write about during grand final week.

Provan really had more pressing concerns than playing silly buggers. When it came to injuries everyone thought of the Sea Eagles but Cronulla had their own injury worries – even though they'd had a long break since their last match.

Fullback Mullane had been carrying a groin injury all year and it had started to get worse at the wrong end of the season. So bad that he'd be getting needled up before the grand final.

There were also concerns with prop Gary Stares, who had injured a shoulder in the major semi against Wests. Provan took a very unusual step to ensure the prop's match fitness; choosing to use himself as a tackling bag. The 10-time premiership winner – who was 45 and had played his last game 13 years ago – ran at Stares and was tackled over and over. Provan did it because he didn't expect Stares' shoulder would survive the session.

"And I didn't want one of the players putting him out of the match and feeling bad about it," the coach said. "I made him tackle me in quick succession and he hit me hard – it was real grand final type work."

There was some good news in the Cronulla pack, in the form of Eric Archer's comeback story. The second-rower had injured his elbow in a trial match against the Dragons at the start of the year. The initial prognosis was a dislocation but after the surgery, Archer found he'd ripped right through his elbow joint. The docs said he'd be out for two seasons. But Archer was having none of that

"I started working on the injury three weeks after it happened," he said. "I did everything from weightlifting to swimming to help strengthen the arm." He even ditched his job as a car salesman and became a labourer to give the arm even more of a workout. It paid off; he worked his way back into the team just before the finals and now was about to play in the grand final.

There was a similar good news story over at Manly as well. Robust winger Stephen Knight's two-year deal with the Tigers had ended last season and he felt he'd had enough of rugby league.

"Training had become a real grind and I was looking everywhere for a way out," he said. "I decided to give football a big miss and pack my boots away for good."

That's when Arthurson came calling, convinced the 29-year-old's career wasn't over. He dangled a one-year deal in front of Knight, who decided to bite – and here he was playing in his first ever grand final.

Also in the Manly camp was an early sign of the concussion issue that has now changed the game for the better. Terry Randall (who had received the first perfect 10 from *Rugby League Week* earlier in the year) was a walk-up starter for the Kangaroo tour at the end of the season but during grand final week he told Kevin Humphreys he wouldn't be going.

"I'm worried about being knocked out," Randall said. "I need a rest and a summer in the sun with my family. I play the game hard but lately I seem to be battered around a bit more than is good for you.

"A couple of times this season I thought of having a

brain scan after being knocked out but have quickly improved and not bothered going ahead with the check."

In terms of match tactics, Manly was playing its cards close to its chest. They even went to the extent of setting up a "secret" training venue for the week. "We want to keep the pressure and exposure of publicity away from the players for the rest of the week," Stanton said. "There's no way anybody will find us at training this week."

Provan had no fear of talking tactics. As well as spending the week playing ducks and drakes with the team selection, he wanted to see his team put Eadie under pressure with high kicks. Provan was convinced the fullback was carrying a back injury into the match and wanted to give him something to think about. It had marked a change in tactics; unlike other teams the Sharks had used the bomb sparingly, preferring to score tries through their speed.

The Sharks coach also wanted to see his players get stuck in should Manly bring the biff. "If they turn on the biff then we'll go along with them," Provan said. "We want a good, fast, open game but are prepared to play it any way it comes."

Sharks hooker John McMartin, the best ball-winner

1978

in the league, also tried to get inside Hartley's head by complaining about the way the ref let Manly half Steve Martin feed the scrums in last week's final. "If the halfback is allowed to get away with anything I lose my advantage," McMartin said.

"I want the ball fed fairly by both halfbacks. All anyone wants is a 50-50 chance of getting the ball. It's been Rafferty's rules with the half feeding the scrum winning the ball."

In a sign that the 1970s were a different era for rugby league, that the grand final would be broadcast live on TV was deemed front-page news the day before the game. As hard as it is to fathom for today's fans, the league had been genuinely considering permitting only a delayed broadcast of the decider at 6pm, because ticket sales a week out weren't what was expected.

In that last week the ticket sales must have improved to give the league comfort in allowing the grand final to go out live. There's a chance a lot of them were bought by Channel 7; the broadcaster was so keen to get the rights to show the game live that it promised to buy any outstanding tickets.

Something else that was common during grand final

week at the time was newspapers calling up various famous people to get their tips. Premier Neville Wran felt the match would be close but was tipping the Sharks, as was Opposition Leader Peter Coleman. Former Test captain Bob Simpson was also a Sharks man, because "they are more consistent that their opponents".

In the Manly camp was NSW Police Commissioner Merv Wood, who liked "their speed and all-round enthusiasm". Judy Lynne, a star of popular soapie *The Young Doctors*, was also backing the Sea Eagles. "If I don't say that my neighbours will give me a nice old pummelling." TV personality Jeannie Little was also going with Manly because "they're much better than those dreadful Sharks".

Reading the papers the day after the drawn grand final the clear consensus was that the game was a dud. "I wasted yesterday watching the tamest, most unimaginative grant final of recent years," wrote journalist Frank Crook. Former player Bob Fulton branded it "duller-than-death"; it was hard to find anyone who had a kind word to say about the match.

But that's usually the way when defence trumps attack. When a team scores it makes the pulse race.

1978

Defence, on the other hand, is viewed as ruining the party; it's stopping everyone from seeing tries being scored.

Sure, that the only scores in the first half were penalty goals (2/2 to Rogers, 1/3 from Eadie) leading to a 4-2 scoreline at the break that didn't look impressive. But there was still plenty to like in the first half. The Sharks scrambling defence was impressive; twice the Sea Eagles put on an expansive backline movement where the ball found winger Mooney. On the first time the sliding goal-line defence of the Sharks bundled him through the black-and-white striped corner post and into touch. The second time the defenders hounded him to the edge, forcing him to put a foot into touch. The Sharks defence on their line was strong, and defence is half the game, regardless of what cranky pundits filing to a deadline claim.

There were also moments of great attack; including those two near tries to Mooney. Late in the half Sharks half Hansard found some space and offloaded to Rogers who loomed up in support. He sped across the halfway and the only defender in front of him was Eadie on the quarter-line. Surprisingly, rather than take on the fullback with his speed, Rogers slowed up and started looking for a supporting team-mate. That left the way open for Eadie to absolutely smash Rogers and take the ball off him. The Sharks centre spent the next few tackles lying on the SCG turf rather than being in the defensive line.

Five minutes into the second half Eadie levelled the score with a penalty goal. Then, in the 51st minute came the moment many Sharks fans felt locked up the match. With Eadie in the line, Rogers put up a bomb which was allowed to bounce. Winger Steve Edmonds had chased through and grounded the ball. With Rogers' conversion the Sharks went up 9-4.

Any feelings of grand final joy from the Sharks fans were short-lived. A few minutes later Randall put up a towering bomb that Mullane failed to reel in (in part because of heavy attention from defenders). Edmonds, the hero just a few minutes earlier, tried to knock the ball over the line but only succeeded in putting in closer to Mooney, who finally got his try. The conversion levelled the score again at 9-all, before the Sea Eagles took the lead with a penalty goal.

It looked done and dusted for the Sharks until Hartley awarded the Sharks a scrum penalty within kicking distance (this being an era where penalty goals were allowed from scrum penalties. And an era where they still had scrum penalties). And Rogers' kick was

1978

straight and true – the scores were locked up again. (as an aside, if Hartley really was pushing for Manly to win as the conspiracy goes, why would he award this penalty and give the Sharks a chance to draw level?).

With the scores deadlocked and eight minutes on the clock, the field goal was the obvious option. Rogers and Steve Martin both had shots, and both missed. When the final siren sounded, the thing that had happened for the first time in 1977 – a drawn grand final – had happened again just 12 months later.

Grand Final Replay

Cronulla vs Manly

Sydney Cricket Ground

Tuesday, September 19

The *Sun-Herald*'s front page headline the day after the drawn grand final said it all – "No! It's on again". It captured the shock and dismay of the decider ending in a draw for the second year in a row. The league copped it for having scrapped the extra time concept this year, many of the pundits conveniently ignoring they had complained about the use of extra time just 12 months earlier. The outcry after the 1977 grand final, along with medical reports that extra time was a danger to players,

1978

fuelled the league's decision to opt for a replay in the event of a drawn grand final.

Two of those people who now disliked the scrapping of extra time were the secretaries of Manly and Cronulla. Ken Arthurson planned to move a motion at the league's general committee meeting that 10 minutes each way be played in the unlikely event of the replay also ending in a draw.

"We must get a result," he said. "It can't keep on." The Sharks' Arthur Winn was singing the same tune. "We'll assist in any way as long as we get a result," he said. "I'm sure the attitude of everyone in rugby league is the same."

That motion of Arthurson's didn't get up; the league committee decided against extra time if scores were level after the replay. Instead, they decided to create the most unusual precedent that Cronulla and Manly would be joint premiers in the event of a draw on Tuesday night.

In truth, extra time is always a better option than a replay; if the league got anything wrong it was in ots knee-jerk response in 1977 to scrap extra time. The core of the problem in 1977 was not the rules, it was the fact that neither St George or Parramatta could score so much as a field goal in the 20 minutes after full-time.

In 1978, the drawn grand final created an extra

headache for the league. There was a Kangaroo team to select, which was scheduled to happen after the weekend's Sydney and Brisbane grand finals. After full-time on Saturday, there was a series of hurried telephone hook-ups where it was decided to delay the selection until after the replay.

It also pushed back the day the tourists would leave, from the Sunday after the grand final weekend to a few days later. That meant the league had to reschedule flights and hotel bookings for the whole team; something that is a hassle now in the age of the internet but was so much worse when it had to all be done over the phone.

At full-time on Saturday, the players were left on the field fuming while Hartley and the linesmen immediately made a bee-line for the sheds. They wanted to keep playing. "What do they think we are – bloody machines?", asked Randall, who no doubt wanted the season to be over already. In the sheds after the drawn decider, he was battered and bruised with bags of ice on his shoulder, right knee, left ankle and right thigh.

Manly five-eighth Ian Martin even looked to stage an on-field protest. "It's a joke – let's stay right here," he said he told the players after the siren sounded. "No-one moved and had Hartley stayed I'm sure we would have got our protest over. I've played in five grand finals now and can't remember a bigger foul-up." Captain Krilich probably didn't have the breath to complain; suffering from a bad case of the flu in the days before the game, he was hooked up to an oxygen mask in the dressing room after the match.

Probably the only person at the SCG who was happy to have a replay was Provan. "We were lucky to get out of it with a draw," he said. "It wasn't one of our better performances and I was happy when the match ended."

That Kangaroo tour ruled out any chance of a replay the following weekend, instead the league had to resort to the unattractive option of holding the biggest game of the season on a Tuesday afternoon, while almost everyone was at work.

An industry group figured that wouldn't stop footy fans; it predicted up to 30,000 people would be calling in sick on Tuesday. "It would have been better if the replay was held next Saturday," said NSW Regional Chamber of Commerce and Industry president Robert Dewley. He estimated the cost to business of those sickies would be around $1.5 million. He was pretty close to the mark when it came to the crowd figure – 33,552 people managed to find their way to the Sydney Cricket Ground for the Tuesday 3.15pm kick-off.

The Tuesday replay meant it was a very short turnaround – for the players and for the media needing to find another few days' worth of stories. Luckily for the sports journos, there was another controversy to splash across the sports pages between Sunday and Tuesday.

Around 15 minutes into Saturday's grand final John Harvey levelled Steve Kneen, leaving him lying on the ground with blood coming from a facial wound. Hartley called the tackle around the shoulders, which replays showed was wrong; Harvey may have used his chest for the tackle, but there was the issue of his raised left forearm which looked to have hit Kneen in the face. It wasn't the same as the Sorenson tackle that saw the Sharks enforcer suspended in the last round of the season, but it wasn't all that far off. To say it was across the chest and award not so much as a penalty was a clear mistake from Hartley. To allegedly tell Cronulla players that Kneen's injuries were from a previous incident didn't help matters.

The Sharks were understandably infuriated; they had lost Sorenson and Pierce to suspension for head-high tackles, yet when one of theirs was on the receiving end, nothing happened.

It highlighted an inconsistency in the league's use of

video evidence. If it worked in their favour – such as citing Wests players for brawling after the Lidcombe match against Manly – then the league was happy to use it. But they weren't keen on using video replays to pick up illegal tackles, even when they had been clearly seen by everyone watching on TV at home.

Though while the Sharks were on the wrong end this time, they – and Kneen himself – had benefited from it a few weeks earlier. In that last-round match, in the very play where Sorenson hit Boyd high, Kneen laid a worse hit on Wests' Geoff Foster but got away scot-free. Even though it had been captured by the TV cameras. If justice had played out then, Kneen wouldn't have been on the field to get whacked by Harvey; he'd have been suspended.

Provan had complained about Hartley missing the Harvey incident, and his referring in general, and refs' boss Eric Cox had had enough of it. The head of the referees clearly felt there was no need for him to show any sense of impartiality and so he went on a very unprofessional rant on the back page of the *Daily Mirror* the day before the replay.

"I refereed Provan as a player – he whinged then and nothing is different now that he's coach," Cox said. "I just wish he'd shut up." Also, even though the TV footage was available for Cox to see where Harvey's forearm went, his research into the incident was limited to asking Hartley what happened and then accepting the ref's response wholesale.

The referee's boss was solely responsible for appointing the officials to each match. Which means Cox was the one who kept picking Hartley week after week. He would have surely been feeling the pressure from having his No1 referee making so many obvious mistakes. And then he made one of his own by lashing out at a coach who was only commenting on what everyone could see on their TV screens.

In an interesting aside, at the end of the season, the Referees Association voted to approach the league to devise a new way of selection officials; they weren't happy that one man – in the 1978 season it was Cox – had total control over their refereeing careers. Some were still unhappy about Hartley's sudden ascension and former No1 Jack Danzey being quickly demoted to reserve grade. By the way, Hartley voted in favour of the decision to create a new selection panel – make of that what you will.

The very day of the replay, *The Sun* carried comments from Sharks secretary Arthur Winn that implied the Cronulla side were expecting to get some sort of free hit

1978

– quite literally. He felt the Sharks should be able to whack someone about the head and not get marched.

"If it was alright on Saturday, it should be okay today," Winn said. "If one Manly forward could get away with a head-high tackle on Saturday, you can't expect the same referee to send one of ours off if such an incident happened."

The odds were against a Sharks win before the opening kick-off, with four players not fit to back up. Fullback Mullane, who had been getting needles in an injured groin for weeks, had finally had enough – the painkillers had worn off halfway through the grand final. Five-eighth Barry Andrews was also out, as was Gary Stares (who had played every finals match as Sorenson's replacement).

The biggest loss was highly-rated hooker McMartin. A strong ball-winner in an era where scrums were a contest, he'd more than held his own against Kangaroos incumbent Max Krilich. He'd injured his knee late in the grand final and, with just a few days between the grand final and the replay, Provan wasn't prepared to give McMasters the chance to prove his fitness, ruling him out on Sunday morning. In his place was lower grade player Rowland Beckett, who would play his first top grade match in the grand final replay.

On top of those four players, the Sharks were also missing Sorenson and Pierce through suspension. While much of the focus was on Manly's walking wounded throughout the grand final charge, it was really the Sharks who were now in trouble. The short turnaround benefitted Manly's aches and pains; the longer the gap between matches, the more time for soreness to take hold. And so they also had the luxury of naming an unchanged line-up for the replay.

It would be a miracle if the Sharks managed to win their first grand final in 1978. That miracle never happened. After an early period where both sides made plenty of errors, Manly were the first to find their rhythm, putting on two impressive tries to Gartner and one to Eadie to have all but wrapped up the premiership with a 15-0 half-time score. The dark clouds that had been coming over the SCG during the first half reflected the mood of the Cronulla fans and the pelting rain in the second stanza made it impossible for the Sharks to mount any sort of comeback. In the first-half scrums Manly's Krilich had outplayed his inexperienced opponent, beating Beckett 7-1 and helping to pave the way for that insurmountable half-time lead.

The only score in the second half was a field goal to Eadie late in the game. There wasn't any need for it;

1978

Manly had the game well and truly won by then – but it took the final score to 16-0. Then Eadie tried another field goal and then Steve Martin went for one too – both missing. In a finals series still dogged by controversy to this day, the totally unnecessary field goal shots in the last minutes of a match already decided never rate a mention. Why add a point or two to the scoreline when, at 15-0, it was all wrapped up?

Speaking of controversy, it turned out Hartley had allowed another Manly try on the seventh tackle. Stephen Knight was tackled on what was the sixth tackle, but instead of a scrum, Hartley allowed him to play the ball. The play went out to the far side, the ball finding Eadie steaming in from the backfield. After skittling a few Sharks, he offloaded a shaky pass to Gartner who had the line right in front of him. On top of that tackle miscount, the Sharks were adamant Gartner was standing offside when he got that final pass. In partial defence of Hartley he had disallowed a try to Manly minutes earlier due to a forward pass in almost identical circumstances, so he wasn't prepared to overlook a forward pass to give the Sea Eagles a try. Yet another botched tackle count was more a sign of a referee with patchy technical skills rather than any deliberate conspiracy.

Regardless of your opinions on Manly, the 1978 premiership was an impressive feat. They had to make it through six finals matches – all but one sudden-death – in 24 days. They had to back up twice to play a mid-week replay after the league's foolish decision to scrap extra time. They also had to play 28 matches in 1978 – two more than grand final opponents Cronulla.

"I've had some thrills in rugby league as a player and a coach but none can come near the feeling of pride I had when the full-time bell rang out," Frank Stanton wrote in the *Big League* annual.

"It was the end of what most people termed the impossible. I have never been associated with a side with such a determined will to win."

If the league thought that full-time bell in the replay would signal an end to the controversy Hartley's performances had stirred up, they were wrong.

Three days after the replay, Souths coach Jack Gibson said his team would refuse to play any game under the referee. "I don't believe what happened in the finals should be allowed to rest – for the sake of the game," Gibson said. "If Hartley had one of Souths' matches next year I don't want my team playing. It's as simple as that."

It was a call backed by Wests' coach Masters. It was

1978

a pretty safe call by Gibson; with Souths finishing ninth in 1979, it was highly unlikely the league's top-rated referee would get a Rabbitohs match. As for Wests, Hartley had them twice in the regular season, twice in the Amco Cup – and all four matches went ahead, despite any bluster from Masters the year before.

Of the top five in 1978, it would only be the premiers who missed out on the finals the following year. Manly let in more points than they scored and finished seventh, three points away from fifth spot. For the record, they only had Hartley four times, winning three of them.

The only newcomer was St George, who finished in top spot and won the premiership. Parramatta had continued to build towards what would be a dominating 1980s, finishing second on the ladder and losing the final to Canterbury. The Dogs managed to make the grand final from fifth spot, the other team who was steadily preparing for its 1980s spotlight.

Cronulla was back in the finals in 1979 but lost both of their matches. They would miss out in 1980 and be back in 1981 but then not taste the finals until 1988. After 1978 it would be 19 years before the Sharks made it to another decider, losing the sole Super League premiership to Brisbane in 1997. It was 38 years after the 1978 disappointment before Sharks fans were able to enjoy grand final victory, defeating the dreaded Storm in 2016.

As for Western Suburbs, the promise offered by 1978 soon faded away to years of mediocrity – or worse. They made the post-season in 1979, 1980 and 1982 – the best result in 1980 when they reached the final. Between 1982 and the merger with Balmain in 1999 the Magpies had just three finals campaigns, generally getting bundled out in the first week. They had become better known for winning wooden spoons – six of them since 1983 – than premierships. For many Wests fans, 1978 was special because it was the last time their team really mattered and was a threat.

Bibliography

Books

Adams, Tony, *Masters of the Game*, Ironbark, 1996
Apter, Jeff, *The Coaches*, Five Mile Press, 2014
Burnett, Adam, and Logue, Matt, *Eelectric: The Story of the Parramatta Eels Golden Years*, New Holland, 2013
Collis, Ian, and Whiticker, Alan, *Rugby League Through the Decades*, New Holland, 2011
Collis, Ian, and Whiticker, Alan, *The History of Rugby League Clubs*, New Holland, 2014
Collis, Ian and Whiticker, Alan, *Tommy: The Extraordinary Career of Tom Raudonikis*, New Holland, 2021
Connolly, Paul (ed), *Rugby League's Greatest Hits*, Hardie Grant, 2013
Chesterton, Ray, *Manly Sea Eagles: The Team They Love To Beat*, New Holland, 2016
Evans, Will, *A Short History of Rugby League in Australia*, Slattery Media Group, 2012
Evans, Will, *Rugby League Rivalries*, Echo, 2015

Fellows, Warren, and Marx, Jack, *The Damage Done*, Pan Macmillan, 1997

Haddan, Steve, *The Finals: 100 Years of National Rugby League Finals*, Steve Haddan, 1992

Hauser, Liam, *The Great Grand Finals; Rugby League's Greatest Contests*, New Holland 2017

Heads, Ian, and Middleton, David, *A Centenary of Rugby League*, Pan Macmillan, 2008

Humphries, Glen, *Biff: Rugby League's Infamous Fights*, Gelding Street Press, 2022

Humphries, Glen, *Jack Gibson's Fur Coat*, Gelding Street Press, 2023

Lester, Gary, *Clouds of Dust, Buckets of Blood*, Playwright Publishing, 1995

Middleton, David (ed), *Rugby League Week: 25 Sensational Years*, HarperSports, 1995

Webster, Andrew, *Supercoach: The Life and Times of Jack Gibson*, Allen and Unwin, 2011

Weber, Therese, and Simpkin, Julie (eds), *League of Legends*, National Museum of Australia Press, 2008

Whiticker Alan, *Mud, Blood and Beer: Rugby League in the 1970s*, New Holland, 2014

Whiticker, Alan, and Hudson, Glen, *The Encyclopedia*

1978

of Rugby League Players, Gary Allen, 1999

Newspapers and magazines
Big League
Canberra Times
Rugby League Week
Sunday Mirror
Sun-Herald
Sunday Telegraph
Sydney Daily Mirror
Sydney Morning Herald
Sydney Sun

www.ingramcontent.com/pod-product-compliance
Lightning Source LLC
Chambersburg PA
CBHW042343300426
44109CB00049B/2780